"Corinne Chilstrom has given us a rare gift: an honest, moving and wonderfully readable account of the experience that must be the hardest in the world for any loving parent. But more than that, she has shared with us the wisdom of a Christian who learns not to flee from death, but facing it, finds even in that feared place the Author of life."

Douglas John Hall
Author of *God and Human Suffering*

"This is a sad, courageous, and inspiring book by an adoptive mother who has experienced every parents' worst fear—the suicide of her child. By bravely taking us on her journey through grief and the struggle to fathom her son's sense of abandonment, hopelessness, and not belonging in the world, Corinne Chilstrom helps us understand the hidden trauma that adopted children carry. Her book gives adoptive families the chance to hear their children's cry for help, and gives meaning to Andrew's life and death."

Betty Jean Lifton
Author of *Lost and Found: The Adoption Experience*

"As a father who also lost a son, I was deeply moved by *Andrew, You Died Too Soon* (and like Andrew, I, too, am adopted). I wept as I relived the feelings of loving and losing. I found Corinne Chilstrom's story to be honest. Deep. Realistic and thoughtful. Hopeful. I trust many parents and others who have lost and those who want to help those who have lost will read it and find help from God in the healing of his wounded people."

Leighton Ford
Leighton Ford Ministries

"In Corinne Chilstrom's book, *Andrew, You Died Too Soon*, we have a mother's telling of her grief and her handling of that grief. As a mother who lost a son, I know how helpful such a book can be to many of us, both in our own sorrow and in how we can help someone else in their time of need."

Nora Rogness
Speaking for herself and her late husband Alvin Rogness

"With startling boldness, Corinne Chilstrom constructed a glass house into which all may see. For the sympathetic observer, she details the horror of suicide and enigmas of adoption, patiently teaching as well. To the helpless onlooker, she offers practical encouragement to become involved with friends in their tragedies. Through it all she carries on a deep conversation about her struggles and triumphs—and our own."

I. Shelby Andress
Search Institute

Andrew, You Died Too Soon

A Family Experience
of Grieving
and Living Again

Corinne Chilstrom

Augsburg
MINNEAPOLIS

ANDREW, YOU DIED TOO SOON
A Family Experience of Grieving and Living Again

Scripture quotations are from the New Revised Standard Version Bible, copyright © 1989 by the Division of Christian Education of the National Council of the Churches of Christ in the United States of America. Used with permission.

The text of the appendix is reprinted by permission of the Rev. Dennis J. Johnson, Gustavus Adolphus College, St. Peter, Minn.

Interior design: Peregrine Publications
Cover design: Peggy Lauritsen Design Group
Cover photo: Herbert W. Chilstrom

Library of Congress Cataloging-in-Publication Data

Chilstrom, E. Corinne, 1931-
    Andrew, you died too soon : a family experience of grieving and living again / E. Corinne Chilstrom.
        p.   cm.
    Includes bibliographical references.
    ISBN 0-8066-2684-4
    1. Consolation. 2. Bereavement—Religious aspects—Christianity.
3. Chilstrom, Andrew. 4. Chilstrom, E. Corinne, 1931- .
5. Chilstrom, Herbert W., 1931- . 6. Lutherans—United States—
Biography. 7. Adoptees—United States—Biography. 8. Teenagers—
Suicidal behavior. I. Title.
BV4907.C48 1993
248.8'6—dc20   93-28083
                                                                        CIP

The paper used in this publication meets the minimum requirements of American National Standard for Information Sciences—Permanence of Paper for Printed Library Materials, ANSI Z329.48-1984.   ∞™

Manufactured in the U.S.A.   AF 9-2684

97   96   95   94   4   5   6   7   8   9   10

Contents

Cover Photo

From the moment I first caught a glimpse of those bright eyes at the adoption agency I started snapping pictures of Andrew. Over the next eighteen years there would be hundreds of them, each capturing a small piece of what promised to be a wonderful life.

I could not have known that the one I took of him on that late August afternoon in 1984 would be the last.

Our rustic summer cabin on Lake Lida was one of Andrew's favorite places. For hours he would wade in the shallow weed beds along shore or stand on the dock casting for bass and pan fish.

Thunderstorms in the late afternoon are common at the end of hot August days. This one was especially violent, sending bolts of lightning streaking across the sky and reflecting in the water. Loud claps of thunder echoed through the hills.

The dark, foreboding clouds were still high in the sky that afternoon when suddenly the setting sun broke through on the western horizon. Its rays illuminated the distant shore. I ran for my camera. There would be only a few minutes to take advantage of the light.

Andrew was already on the dock with his fishing gear when I focused the camera. He stood in the shadows; on the far hills the sun was having the last word.

Despair and hope; sorrow and joy; darkness and light.

"If I say, 'Surely the darkness shall cover me, and the light around me become night,' even the darkness is not dark to you; the night is as bright as the day, for darkness is as light to you" (Psalm 139:11-12).

Herbert W. Chilstrom

Foreword

Acquainted with sorrow, the author shares her grief, invites others into the circle of mourners, offers quiet counsel on grieving to others who need it and welcome it—and still succeeds in having written an affirmative book.

The most hardened readers are not likely to get past page two or three without finding their eyes blurring with tears, or to be able to read through all the pages without finding them welling up from time to time. But don't each of us have enough disappointments, shadows, and difficulties sustaining morale even on good days, to say nothing of occasions for sorrow in bad seasons, to find reason to avoid having to take on the burdens of such a story?

Yes: we do have our problems and traumas. But it is the author's intent that reading this will be an experience which enhances life; one which will help make the encounter with grief not only more bearable, but actually growth-producing. Readers will find here therapy, catharsis, understanding, and even fresh grounding for faith, hope, and love—hope, being at such times and momentarily, "the greatest of these."

Why? Many of us, without knowing the source, may share the theory that writers of autobiographical material should remember that the reader will not implicitly be saying, "Tell me about you!" Instead they will be thinking: "Tell me about me, using your experience as a model or example." So it is here: tell us, author Corinne Chilstrom, about the resources on which I and mine can draw in times of crises. Tell us, author, you who for the moment become Everyparent: tell us about the tears of God, the strength of a love that will not let us go when our anger wells up. Tell us about how faith upholds you when doubt and despair would overwhelm. Tell us about hope and how it will outlast the bleakness of shock that comes with the worst things that can happen to those around us. Tell us. She does.

A final word about the style of the book. I note that with forthright candor, Corinne Chilstrom lets her outreach to certain special readers break through her narrative and reflections. She names names of people who formed the company of burden bearers and tells how they lightened hers. She sends explicit cards of thanks, so direct and to the point that no editor would have penciled them out as being disruptive to plot or unfitting. With this device, she shows us how grief and joy in the abstract are thin and passing, but deep sorrows and rich exaltations are concrete. They get associated with real names, as they should: Corinne, Herb, their Jesus, specific congregations. And Andrew. Who died too soon.

Martin E. Marty
The University of Chicago

A Note to the Readers

Many people already know Corinne and Herbert Chilstrom. For those who do not, we thought it appropriate to provide some information about them.

Corinne Chilstrom's first career was as a registered nurse, working in several specialties including pediatrics, medical-surgical nursing, and hospice. Corinne and Herbert Chilstrom were married in 1954 and have three children, Mary, Chris, and Andrew. Corinne studied for the ministry and was ordained in 1985. She served Bethlehem Lutheran Church in Minneapolis from 1985 to 1987, and is currently serving St. Luke's Lutheran Church in Park Ridge, Illinois.

Herbert Chilstrom was ordained in 1958 and served Lutheran congregations in Minnesota and was a professor and academic dean at Luther College in Teaneck, New Jersey. From 1976 to 1987 he was bishop of the Minnesota Synod of the Lutheran Church in America, and in 1987 was elected presiding bishop of the Evangelical Lutheran Church in America. He currently holds that position.

1.
Our Story
of Grief

It is now eight years since our son died. The grief has been excruciating. My husband Herb and I have chosen to be open with our grief experience. As a result, since our son's death other parents who lost children have often opened their hearts to us as they reached out for someone to understand.

I offer our story of grief primarily for parents who grieve the loss of a child. It is my hope that our story will spark in you the reality, the depth of your loss. And that you will meet in these pages the one who is a "man of sorrows and acquainted with grief," who offers help to lift your burden and sweeten your sorrow, help to *grieve and live again.*

Second, I write to honor those who held us up when our world fell apart. You held us together by giving of yourselves in so many ways. Coming quickly when we needed you. Hugs and hot dishes. Tears and telephone calls. Listening, listening, listening to our words of sorrow. Your presence was life-sustaining. You have been "the body of Christ" for us. Through you, we have felt the heartbeat of God's steadfast love. You have helped us *grieve and live again.*

Third, I write for you who believe that it is weak to grieve and that you must hide your grief. Whatever your losses, you have tried to ignore the painful emotions necessary to grieve. Sorrow, instead of flowing outward, has become stagnant within you—a destructive force. Harmful to you and to those you love. I offer this book with the hope that long after your loss you may even now *grieve and live again.*

2.
Oh, My God!

Corinne, this almost sounds like a suicide note," Herb said as he handed me the piece of paper.

He had finished dressing before I did, and went downstairs. The borrowed van in the driveway was full of wood for the fireplace. Dressed in old clothes, we planned to unload the van before calling Andrew for breakfast. Then we would go to church together.

It was a crisp fall morning in Minnesota. The frost that covered the bleak November landscape was quickly giving way to the early warmth of the sun. The kind of day when even an icy soul would yield to the brightness of the day.

I sat on the edge of the bed tying my shoes, happy that Andrew was home from college for the weekend, when I heard Herb's quick steps on the stairs. He paused in the doorway. Fear was in his face.

"Something is really strange," he said. "Andrew isn't in his room. The television was on. Lights on all over the place. And I found this note by the phone."

Hurriedly, I read it. A poem. Hidden meanings. "So much I lose." It did sound like a suicide note. Where was he? Urgency gripped me, too. I followed Herb down the stairs all the way to the basement. The lights were on down there, too.

At the landing, Herb stopped abruptly as though something had hit him. He leaned against the wall. His face blanched. "Oh, my God!"

14

Frightened, I hesitated. Yet, I had to see what he saw. As I took another step cautiously, Herb's hand held me back. "Don't look! He shot himself!"

I both had to and didn't dare to look. So I saw just a little of what he saw. Andrew lay on the floor. I saw only his legs—he was wearing his favorite old khaki pants and black hightop canvas shoes.

Grasping each other on the landing, we stood immobilized. Herb moaned. "Oh, Andrew. Andrew. Andrew." It was the moaning of a father who loved so much. Who was loved so much.

How long we stood there holding each other up, I don't know. And I don't know how we stumbled on lifeless legs to the couch in the family room. There we sat, holding each other, sobbing and stunned.

The morning sun streamed through the large picture window. It should have made us warm and glad. Icy cold and shivering, I was unable to let the sun's rich rays touch me. Trembling, we held each other tightly.

"We have to call the police," Herb said at last.

"We need to call friends first," I answered.

Neither of us could move. Nothing seemed real. Not even our own bodies. Suddenly the desperate reality of our need for support overwhelmed me. Feeling a rush of adrenalin, I flew to the phone and made three frantic calls.

"Come right away. Something terrible has happened!" Beside me, Herb took the phone and called his two sisters. "Come right away. Andrew shot himself."

Then he made the dreaded call to the police station.

Herb sank into a chair beside the kitchen table and I sat on his lap. Waiting. The coldness I felt was like nothing I had ever known before. My body was shaking uncontrollably. I needed to be held tightly. My teeth chattered. I didn't dare leave Herb's clutch, nor he mine. That's where we were when everyone came.

3.
Is He Dead?

They came so quickly, the two police officers. Our knees felt like they would collapse, and we made it to the front door only by holding each other. "Our son. He's in the basement. He shot himself!" They went downstairs while we sat down on the kitchen chair. One of them came back and stood in the doorway. I jumped up and stood face to face with the officer, forcing my words. Frantically I asked, "Is he dead?"

As a nurse, I had helped many people to die. When injured, some die quickly. Some linger. From the look on Herb's face there on the landing, I knew Andrew must be dead, but my heart refused to believe it. So many questions. It couldn't be possible. Athletic and full of life. Since he was an infant in arms, he'd hugged me so tightly. And as a teenager he was quick to hug me even when his friends were around. He'd done that just the night before. His friends came for him, and just before going out the door with them he turned and embraced me. "I love you, Andrew." "And I love you, Mom." Could he now be lifeless? Hoping against hope, I had to ask, "Is he dead?"

Looking deep into my pleading eyes, the officer gave me the dreaded answer. "Yes, he is dead." That sentence changed our lives.

Dead. Andrew dead. As long as we live, we will never have him again. How could I, why should I live without him? All of the work and love of mothering him, lost! These thoughts welled up within me like a volcano ready to explode. I turned, bursting with anger. Pounding the kitchen table with my fist, I shouted,

"Adoption! These kids never feel like they really belong in this world. Who will ever understand?" I crumpled on Herb's lap, weeping uncontrollably. Lost in grief, we held each other, joined by the bond of parenting. Remembering. The officer stood beside us, silent.

What a violent reaction! Where did it come from? Why did I blurt out those desperate words? Many adoptees seem to graft easily onto a new family. Little did I know how prophetic those words would be. Nor did I realize that those words would beckon me into a world of discovery. Searching out the special needs of teenage adoptees. Poring over the literature in libraries. Joining adoption groups. Listening—to adoptees searching for their roots; to birth mothers, longing and searching for children they'd given up and could never forget; to adoptive parents needing answers. My desperate words on that desperate day were the volcano that spawned national research on adoption, the first of its kind, seeking to define the special needs of adopted teens and their families.

But back to the officer. He stood there quietly, respectfully. At last and when the time was right, he made his request. "We need to search your house." Certainly there was plenty of evidence that Andrew had taken his own life. But there is a routine that must be followed, and we understood. "Go ahead." He went alone to every room in the house. It felt so strange.

The officer found everything neat and orderly. I had cleaned the house from top to bottom in anticipation of Andrew's visit. Our home felt so cozy and warm when it was in order. Andrew loved it that way and often said, "I don't like to clean, but I really like a clean house." As he perched himself beside me when I baked or cleaned, he'd grin and say, "I'm going to marry a workaholic like you, Mom, so I won't have to work so hard!" Andrew's favorite foods were ready for the weekend. I had baked chocolate chip cookies for him to take back to college. I liked having the work finished when the children came home so we could just enjoy each other. And now our home, all in order, was being inspected for death clues!

In the midst of all this, the coroner arrived. He went to the basement family room where the younger officer had remained with Andrew. I wondered what they were finding, what they were doing to him!

Having finished the house search, the older officer came to us. "I need to ask you some questions." So Herb and I went to the couch by the warm sunny window in the family room. I was frightened. Did he suspect us in some way? Would he be harsh when we felt so shattered? We didn't need to wonder long.

With compassion he began, "I am a parent, too." He hesitated before saying more. I sensed tears in his voice and kindness in his spirit. This uniformed officer was efficient and composed, feeling with us in our sorrow, sensitive to our needs. The coroner, who joined us for more questions, also showed empathy and care.

Meanwhile, Andrew's high school girlfriend, Julie, was driving by. Two years younger than Andrew, she was sixteen and a high school junior. Reluctantly, they'd decided to date others when Andrew started college. As Julie drove down Gleason Road, she was startled to see all the commotion. Right in front of our house stood a police car with flashing red lights and the county coroner's vehicle. "What is happening?" she wondered, feeling frightened. "It couldn't be Andrew. He is down at college. Something terrible must have happened to Herb or Corinne!" She told us later that she had wanted to stop, but instead circled and drove by one more time. When she got home, the telephone rang. It was Don, Andrew's classmate and the last person who had spoken with him, who told her. "Andrew is dead!"

And then Andrew left home for the last time. Wrapped in khaki plastic. His gun and note went with him, also wrapped in plastic. Home. His home. Our home. Love. Life. And now, suddenly, so much loss. So much emptiness. So much grief. "Grief . . . the price we pay for love."[1]

Note

1. Colin M. Parkes, *Bereavement* (New York: International Universities Press, 1972), 5.

4.
Telephone Call

It had been a Thursday evening when the telephone rang. "Hello, Mom, this is Andrew." He was calling from college. "Will you both be home this weekend because I'd like to come home."

"Yes, we'll both be here and we're both free. It'll be so good to see you."

I loved Andrew's phone calls. They were never long. He was always up front about what he needed. From school or a friend's house. From camp or college. "Can you . . .?" "I need . . ." "You won't believe this, but . . ." Precise, to the point.

Friday evening he arrived in time for dinner. Walked in the front door with a small satchel. I asked, "Where are your dirty clothes?"

"There wasn't room in the car."

"But you were only three people."

"Well, I didn't have time to get them together."

Puzzled, I replied, "But you have no classes on Fridays."

"Mom, you worry too much! I'll get them washed. You know what happened to one of my friends the other day? He went down to wash his clothes and had to leave them because all the machines were busy. When he came back the next day, his clothes were not only washed, but dried and folded too! Can you imagine someone doing all of that for you?"

"Yes, I can imagine that! For eighteen years someone has been doing all of that for you!"

19

We had a good laugh. But he insisted, "I mean someone who's not your mom!" Knowing his tendency to be disorganized, I didn't think again about his dirty clothes. He'd manage somehow. It was fun to have him home.

We had good talks that evening and the next day. Plans for the next quarter. Hopes and dreams. It was time to get dressed for going out, but there was one more important concern. He wanted to know how I was doing, often home alone now. And whether I planned to go back to work in a church, because he knew I was happiest then. He pressed me. "I don't want anyone to put you down just because you're a woman, Mom!" That was our last conversation. He cared. We were close.

Saturday when he was out, there were many calls. "Is Andrew there?" A whole list of messages waited for him by the phone.

Later, we knew there had been something very significant about his call on Thursday evening, wanting to come home for the weekend.

Unknown to us, he'd gotten his midterm grades. One was an F. He'd dropped a course and added another. He was floundering and reluctant to go for help. We'd had many discussions about this problem on the telephone. He was proud, and surely felt a sense of failure.

On that same Thursday evening, he'd had a fight with his new college girlfriend. In a rage, he'd exploded, "I'm going home this weekend and kill myself!" He stormed out. She was frightened and got his friends to go searching for him. They looked all over campus and town for Andrew. At last, they gave up and came back to the dorm, where they found him in his room, humorous as usual. No problem, they were convinced, so they didn't tell anyone. They didn't know what I knew—that he'd called asking if it were a good weekend to come home. And I didn't know what they knew—that he'd threatened to go home and kill himself!

The phone went suddenly silent when Andrew died. I miss his friends calling for him. But most of all, I miss Andrew's calls.

TELEPHONE CALL

How I wish I could hear again, "Hello, Mom, this is Andrew." Before saying good-bye in that last phone call, as always, I said, "I love you, Andrew." I wish I could tell him again. And I wish that I could hear again his usual reply, "And I love you too, Mom!"

5.
Run to
the Griever

R un to the griever. Drop everything. Get there as fast as you can, said John Brantner, a University of Minnesota psychologist and specialist in grief seminars.

In desperation, we had made five calls. And those whom we called came quickly, so very quickly! While the coroner and the younger officer were still in the basement with Andrew, and the older officer was searching the house, the relatives and friends we'd summoned so frantically began to arrive.

Marybeth was first. I had just heard the dreaded sentence— "Yes, he is dead." And then I said it myself for the very first time, to Marybeth. "Andrew is dead. He shot himself!" I heard myself say it. Flossie came. Winnie and Clyde. Addie and Earle. And Dee. To each of them Herb and I took turns saying, "Andrew is dead." We needed to say it again and again. Already our heads knew it, but our hearts were a long way from believing it!

What we didn't know was that it would take months, even years, for our hearts to understand. That is the work of grief, to help the heart know what the head knows. That was the task of these early arrivals. To listen. Listen to our words, listen to our swollen hearts. They were there for us. We were no longer alone.

The shock of sudden loss is like an explosion. Being blown apart limb from limb, thought from thought. Outbursts of emotion. Bursting with strange energy one moment and collapsing the next. Disorganized. Broken by shock into mere fragments.

22

And now these first dear ones, hugging, holding the broken pieces of our selves from being lost.

Their hugs already had begun the mending, even in those first excruciating hours. Addie and Earle. Winnie and Clyde. Flossie. Marybeth. Dee. How did they know to come so quickly? Just being there. Their presence brought stability when our world had fallen apart. It seemed as though they had been sent by God and that they brought God to us. Seven of them, like a sacrament.

At some point that morning we made a surprising discovery. Ordinarily, all of them go to nine o'clock Sunday morning worship. But for some reason they had been delayed. Dressed and ready for church, each of them answered when we called, and within seconds were in their cars headed for our home. Later when we wondered about this phenomenal timing we called the police station to check the exact time our call had come in that morning—9:02. All of them should have been gone, but they were right there beside their phones. All of them. Did God intervene in our need? If so, why did God not intervene to stop Andrew from taking his life? I wondered.

Coming must have been hard for them—and all of the things they did that day. For they loved Andrew, too. I couldn't bear to see Andrew carried out, and they shielded me by closing the kitchen door. Before leaving, the coroner asked for paper towels. He did some of the cleanup, but they found towels to wipe Andrew's blood from the carpet. Throughout his life they had prayed for him, given him gifts, laughed and cried with him, and now they performed this labor of love. And we'll never know which towels they used, because Addie took them home to launder. She put them back on the shelf the very next day, saving us from further injury.

Thank you for coming on the run!

6.
Is There Resurrection?

Meanwhile, Herb and I were still in our old clothes, dressed to unload wood before going to church. That had been our plan until everything changed. We didn't even realize what we were wearing. It was Earle who said, "You two go upstairs and clean up. We'll take care of everything." Shock knows not what to do. Earle, we needed you to tell us.

Cold water felt so good on our burning eyes and puffy faces. And then we looked into the mirror. Who were these strangers? We saw them in the mirror, aged and drawn, and said to them, "Our son is dead. Let it be a nightmare that began when we left our room this morning. Let us wake up all over again and find it was only a terrible dream." But we knew that it was no dream. It was real. Our son was dead. We looked at the two people in the mirror. They were different now, and we needed to get reacquainted with them. It would take a long time. Would they ever laugh again? Would they ever love again? we wondered.

It felt good to be alone. We closed our bedroom door. We stood in each other's arms weeping for a long, long time. In silence. We didn't want to face the world, or reality, or responsibility. We wanted to hide together. And in our silence we felt the power of the promise: "The Spirit helps us in our weakness; for we do not know how to pray as we ought, but that very Spirit intercedes with sighs too deep for words" (Rom. 8:26).

Herb spoke first. "Oh, God, is there any resurrection?" We seemed to be waiting for God to answer. We waited a long time, enfolded in each other's arms and in God's. God was weeping with us. And our Risen Lord was there. "God, receive Andrew safe into your everlasting arms."

Knowing we needed to get back downstairs, we went to our closet. What do you wear on such a day? What does it matter? Herb didn't want to shave, and why would I put on make-up? But we did these things because Earle told us to. We did it for Earle. When you're numb with grief, you need an Earle. We felt better when we looked better and when we had found a quiet place alone with God.

7.
Gathering
the Family

How would we get in touch with Mary and Chris? How
would we break the news that their brother was dead?
Who would be with them when they got the news? How would
they get home? Quickly. We needed flight arrangements before
we called. We were frantic to have them home, immobilized at
the prospect of figuring it all out.

Our seven helpers in the kitchen just took over. They'd started
to make phone calls immediately. It was an immense relief to
turn everything over to them. They knew just what to do, and
figured it out together.

Chris was a student at the University of Wisconsin in Madison.
My sister Devona and her husband who lived in Madison were
his godparents. They were called out of church. How good it
was to hear their voices! They would go to Chris's apartment.
How sad it was to imagine Chris hearing the news!

Because Chris and Andrew were four years apart in age, during
adolescence they were not close as brothers. But during Andrew's
last year of high school, Chris moved home to attend the University of Minnesota. That year they became very close. Often
they traded clothes, sometimes without asking. Especially the
new ones! And then I was called upon to referee. "No, you're
big boys now," I would say. "You can figure it out." It was a
friendly battle. They sat up late studying together, enjoying the
same music. They had long talks and learned to know each other
well, proud to be each other's brother. Best friends, there wasn't
anything they wouldn't do for each other. How could Chris live

without Andrew? My heart was breaking with sadness for him, thinking of Devona and Harley knocking on his door. Yet thankful, too, because he was close to them and we knew no one would handle it better.

Mary was in Arizona staying with Jeanne, her best friend from college. At last our faithful helpers got through and had Jeanne on the line. Yes, Mary was there, but she was still asleep. How grateful I felt that Mary was not alone.

"Jeanne," we said, both on the line, "sit down. We have terrible news. Andrew is dead." She knew Andrew and she knew how close Mary felt to him. She was all broken up. Yes, she would help Mary pack and would get her to the airport. There was just time to catch the flight.

"I'll get Mary," said Jeanne.

Mary had had much confusion in her young life. How would she manage this on top of everything else?

"Hello, Mary." She sounded sleepy. "Sit down, Mary," said Herb. "We have some very sad news."

Suddenly her voice sounded tense. "What happened, Dad?"

"Mary, Andrew is dead."

She shouted and cried out, "Andrew, *no, no, no, it can't be!*"

We didn't talk long because she had a lot to do in a short time. And then there were the hours alone on the long flight to Minneapolis. It broke our hearts to think of it.

Time made no sense to me that day. All I know is that the sun was low and rosy in the west when we rode to the airport in the back seat of Ron and Dee's car. First we met Chris, broken up. How good to hug him tight and cry together. Devona was with him. She had known she must drop everything and come with him. Then we met Mary. Poor Mary. Too sad to cry and too tense to hug or be hugged. Her first words were, "I won't go to a funeral." We knew we must go carefully. She had another deep grief, still unresolved. Ever since the adoption agency found her birth mother, who rejected meeting her, Mary had not been herself. Talking. Counseling. Nothing helped. What were we to do now?

Riding home, Devona sat in front with Ron and Dee. Mary, Chris, Herb, and I were together in the back. I felt thankful. We needed each other, and needed to be close. I remember the sky ablaze with red as the sun slipped over the horizon. Its beauty is etched in my memory forever.

Blended with the beauty was a hollow feeling. It was at that moment I realized for the first time how utterly lonely grief can be! Here I was with my family, but I felt alone in the universe. What I had yet to learn was that this overpowering sensation of loneliness would return each time I saw a red sky at sunset. I would need to enlarge my heart, blending beauty and loneliness.

Home. The four of us were together at the end of this longest day of all days. Andrew, the youngest, had always been there when the rest of us were together. Now it seemed so strange that he wasn't there, and that he would never be part of our family circle again. There was so much to share. Details of his coming home for the weekend. What his friends who had come that day had told us. The preparatory dreams three of us had had. Chris's frantic telephone calls to reach Andrew the day before. He didn't know why, but he felt worried for Andrew. None of us had thought of his dying, but somehow we'd each been prepared in different ways. We shared. We needed to be together.

Four nights earlier, Herb had dreamed that he was talking with Mary and Chris about being financially responsible young adults. But Andrew was off to the side. Yet he needed more help than the others. Why had he not been in the circle? Herb asked himself when he awoke.

During the night, Mary had been awake for a long time. It had been very dark in the third-story apartment bedroom where she slept. She was finally sleeping deeply when she was awakened by a stabbing pain in her heart, accompanied by a very bright light. She looked around but couldn't figure out where the light had come from. With a sense of sadness she fell asleep once more, only to be awakened by our call.

I, too, had a dream that night. Walking to my car at dusk in the downtown parking lot at work, I came upon five young men in a huddle. Sensing that something terrible was about to happen,

I turned, retreating into the building. Soon the young men were in the building behind a closed door. Frenzy was building in the circle. I awoke feeling afraid. So afraid that I woke Herb. Never in our married life had I done that before. "I feel afraid, as though something frightening is happening somewhere," I told him. We talked for a long time. The following morning was cheerful and a day of rest. Andrew was home with us. Then we found him, and I knew the meaning of my dream.

Our family, now together, had so much to share. Having lived through this very long day, we learned anew the importance of always leaving a contact point when traveling. Because in a tragedy, family members need each other desperately and immediately.

8.
Pact between Marriage Partners

November 11, 1984. Shattered with loss. Hugged by many. Touched through phone calls by many who cared. One man said, "The only thing I can say is that I'm crying with you." We were thankful for the overwhelming love of friends who brought wonderful food. We were comforted to have Mary and Chris home at last. And we were totally exhausted. What would we have done without our brothers, sisters, and friends? They did everything for us. They made calls, answered phones, took messages, kept track of who brought food and flowers. They set food and drink before us when we'd never have known we needed it. November 11—the longest day of our lives.

Night had fallen. Before our helpers went home for the night, it seemed natural to gather in order to comfort one another. And what better way of doing this than to bring our sorrow to God? With no words of our own to pray, Herb opened our *Lutheran Book of Worship* and led us in prayers for Andrew and for us, with words given us for this night by others long ago.

" 'I am the resurrection and the life,' says the Lord; 'he who believes in me, though he die, yet shall he live, and whoever lives and believes in me shall never die' " (John 11:25-26a, LBW, 210).

"Grant to all who mourn a sure confidence in your loving care, that, casting all their sorrow on you, they may know the consolation of your love" (210).

"Give courage and faith to those who are bereaved, that they may have strength to meet the days ahead in the comfort of a holy and certain hope, and in the joyful expectation of eternal life with those they love" (210).

"Help us, we pray, in the midst of things we cannot understand, to believe and trust in the communion of saints, the forgiveness of sins, and the resurrection to life everlasting" (210).

"God of grace, you sent your Son, our Savior Jesus Christ, to bring life and immortality to light. We give you thanks because by his death Jesus destroyed the power of death and by his resurrection has opened the kingdom of heaven to all believers. Make us certain that because he lives we shall live also, and that neither death nor life, nor things present nor things to come shall be able to separate us from your love which is in Christ Jesus our Lord, who lives and reigns with you and the Holy Spirit, one God, now and forever. Amen" (210).

"O God our Father, your beloved Son took children into his arms and blessed them. Give us grace, we pray, that we may entrust *Andrew* to your never-failing care and love, and bring us all to your heavenly kingdom; through your Son, Jesus Christ our Lord. Amen" (208).

And now the long night lay ahead. Passing Andrew's room, we went in to sit on his empty bed. Oh, Andrew! What longing. So many nights I sat on the edge of this bed reading C. S. Lewis's *Chronicles of Narnia* and J. R. R. Tolkien's *Fellowship of the Ring*. I thought of the evening prayers we said together, always ending with the same words: "Dear God, please help me grow up to be a healthy and a happy Christian boy." A tight hug and a kiss. Love. Such precious memories.

We remembered the day we took Andrew to college, just five weeks earlier. That night we shed tears, too, beside his empty bed. But this was different. His bed was so much emptier tonight. And I was overwhelmed with the feeling that I could not live without him.

We fingered his trophies, lined up on the shelf—football, wrestling, baseball. Memories of going to games. How fleet of foot he was, and how graceful his movements! As a young boy, he'd come to me breathless, gasping, "I just love to run fast!" Testing the ultimate strength of his muscles was his greatest

31

delight—tackling in football, pinning opponents in wrestling, getting his dad on the floor for a good match. When I encouraged him to go out for basketball, he retorted, "No, in basketball you're not allowed to touch anyone, Mom, and I like to cream people!"

Is it possible that this beautiful athletic body now lies limp and dead? No, no, no, it can't be true. And then I voiced my lurking fear. "Will we be able to see him dead? What did he do to himself? Will we be able to have a viewing? Unless we see him dead, can we ever believe that he really died?" Going to our room, we closed the door.

It felt so good to be alone. We were exhausted but couldn't go to sleep. There was still something we needed to get out. *Fear.*

"I feel afraid, Herb."

Tenderly he urged me, "Say more."

Throughout the years I had done a great deal of grief work with people—as a nurse, in hospice situations, through pastoral counseling, in workshops. From my experience with others, I knew one grim fact. Statistics show that more than 70 percent of couples end up divorced after the serious illness or death of a child. One reason is that unlike other losses, both partners are grieving equally. Usually when there is a death, one of the marriage partners is the primary griever and the other one the comforter. But when a child is ill or dies, both parents grieve deeply. Knowing this, I wondered, how will we cope? We are not different from others. Could our marriage be spared this destroying wedge? I felt desperately afraid.

Sitting there that night on the edge of our bed, Herb and I made a pact. It was a vow as important as those spoken to each other thirty years before on our wedding night and has remained as important ever since. We promised each other that whatever our feelings, we would be open and honest in expressing them to each other.

"Herb, may I wake you in the night if I need to talk?" I asked.

"Yes, Corinne, and I will do the same."

Awakened by hearing our name, by a dream, a tug, or by sobs. That was the beginning of many important nighttime conversations. Helping each other empty our feelings. Being hollowed out. Making room for God to work.

We knew so little about good interpersonal communication when we were married. We took advantage of opportunities to learn those skills along the way, and we made some gains. But this course, this honesty with our feelings, this grief journey, was to become the greatest learning experience of all. We've learned to bring our honest feelings to God. To leave them with Jesus at the cross and go away free, again and again. Feeling close to Jesus was the most precious gift of all. Andrew, you would like that, because you felt close to Jesus, too.

9.
Funeral Arrangements

I didn't want to face it! But the fact was, our family now had to plan a funeral—a funeral that would fit our needs. And so each of us needed to say what was important for us.

Herb took the lead, gathering the four of us around the kitchen table. We thought back to the days in the southern Minnesota town of St. Peter where we'd lived before Herb's election to the office of synod bishop; where all of us were an integral part of congregation and community. It was the place where we had known the greatest personal support. It was a place Andrew loved. We decided that was where he should be buried. We needed Dennis, a pastor friend, whose family and ours had bonded together recently at Holden Village—a Cascade Mountain retreat center. The funeral should be at the Gustavus Adolphus College chapel. As these ideas were discussed one by one, we all knew they were right.

Scripture. What word from God did we need most? We would be gathered with those who would help us claim the promises of God. So, carefully, Herb chose them.

"There is therefore now no condemnation for those who are in Christ Jesus . . . Whether we live or whether we die, we are the Lord's" (Rom. 8:1; 14:8).

"Do not let your hearts be troubled. Believe in God, believe also in me. . . . Peace I leave with you; my peace I give to you. I do not give to you as the world gives. Do not let your hearts be troubled, and do not let them be afraid" (John 14:1, 27).

First Lutheran Choir. We had happy memories singing in that choir. Andrew was four years old when we moved to St. Peter, and he'd often tug at my choir robe as he sat beside me in the balcony. Sunday after Sunday, he drew pictures on the bulletin. On St. Michael and All Angels' Day, I remember looking down and seeing a gun sketched into St. Michael's hand! And he would snuggle. Affectionate Andrew! He'd go with me to the communion rail, and there at the altar I would whisper into his ear, "Andrew, Jesus loves you!" Before long he beat me to it. With sparkling eyes he pulled my sleeve and whispered, "Mom, Jesus loves you!" Yes, we need the choir to sing at Andrew's funeral.

Chris wanted the choir to sing "There Is a Balm in Gilead." He'd sung it in the high school concert choir, and it meant a lot to him. The words were important to him, especially now:

There is a balm in Gilead to make the wounded whole.
There is a balm in Gilead to heal the sinsick soul.

Sometimes I feel discouraged an' think my work's in vain
But then the Holy Spirit revives my soul again.

Don't ever feel discouraged, our Father is our friend,
And if we lack for knowledge he'll not refuse to lend.[1]

There is a balm in Gilead to make the wounded whole.
There is a balm in Gilead to heal the sinsick soul.

Mary needed to go by herself to pick out a hymn. Mary. Six years old when Andrew came to be her brother. The little black rocker was where she first held and mothered him. He was a very special little brother. Because his eyes seemed to sparkle in response to her love, she soon began to call him Andrew Bright Eyes. And now those eyes were closed in death. Mary needed to do something for Andrew. And so, alone, she chose the hymn that everyone at the funeral would help us pray for Andrew.

Finish then thy new creation, pure and spotless let it be;
Let us see thy great salvation perfectly restored in thee!
Changed from glory into glory, till in heaven we take our place,

35

Till we cast our crowns before thee, lost in wonder, love, and praise (*LBW*, 315).

Hidden away in my own heart was the song I sang with the children when I tucked them in for the night. I needed to sing it one more time with Andrew. It captures everything—and certainly now. I wanted the choir to sing it just before we left for Andrew's burial.

> Jesus tender shepherd hear me; bless thy little lamb tonight.
> Through the darkness be thou near me; keep me safe 'til morning light.
>
> All this day thy hand has led me and I thank thee for thy care.
> Thou hast clothed me, warmed, and fed me; listen to my evening prayer.
>
> Let my sins be all forgiven; bless the friends I love so well.
> Take us all at last to heaven; happy there with thee to dwell.[2]

Somehow, the dread of planning the service had turned into good grief work as we shared our family memories and our own needs. It was good and necessary to be together in our grieving.

We steeled ourselves for the drive to St. Peter to make further arrangements. We needed to visit the funeral home, to choose a casket for Andrew. No, I couldn't even imagine it!

Notes

1. *Youth's Favorite Songs* (Minneapolis: Augustana Luther League, n.d.), #188.

2. *Service Book and Hymnal* (Minneapolis: Augsburg, 1958), #235.

10.
Bearing One Another's Burdens

I t was late morning when they came, the two former neighbors from St. Peter. As soon as they'd caught wind of how our plans were developing, they came. They'd watched Andrew grow up. One had lived next door. The other was a close family friend. Both were mothers. And today they were sad with us.

But besides sharing our sorrow, they had a mission. Because they knew our hearts turned toward St. Peter where all four of us had known a real sense of community, they wanted to help. Seeing how paralyzed we were, they began to make suggestions. Since the visitation would be Tuesday evening and the funeral Wednesday morning, would we like the college guest house for relatives? One of them invited our family to sleep at her home. She could rally neighbors to bring a potluck dinner so we could eat at her house between the afternoon and evening visitation. Since the service would be at 11:00 A.M., women from the congregation would prepare a lunch at the church. Everything would be seen to. It all seemed overwhelming. But it was clear that we wouldn't need to worry about any of it! As these dear friends left, we knew everything was under control.

That night at the college guest house was a special time for relatives from both sides of our family. It was a time to comfort one another, to enjoy each other, to laugh together.

We received and shared the dinner that neighbors brought for our extended family. Being with them, knowing they had loved Andrew, made us feel warmed and protected.

37

The night at the home of our former neighbor was special as well. She knew we'd be exhausted and wanted to save us the late drive home, and back again early in the morning. She was wise, and it felt good to be safe in the care of good friends for the night.

Later, when we were once again able to function, they gave us a list of people to thank. They had carried the load for us, gotten others to help when we weren't able to help ourselves. Although the burden of sorrow was heavy, we didn't have to bear it alone. We began to understand more than ever before what Paul meant when he wrote, "Bear one another's burdens, and in this way you will fulfill the law of Christ" (Gal. 6:2).

11.
A Sister's Presence

Devona is my sister, four years older than I. We were just enough different in age so we were not close growing up. One of my earliest memories is coloring orange on every page of her new coloring book while she was in school. From her I learned the word *trespass*. We slept together in the same brown metal bed. She counted out the spokes of the headboard and told me, "This is your limit, don't trespass!"

Mostly, that was what our relationship was like until I was eighteen and entered nursing school at the hospital where she was already a respected surgical nurse. There, for the first time, we became good friends. We were in each other's weddings. We were mothers together. We shared treasured visits. Even across the miles, our relationship was one of knowing what was needed, of standing by, of loving and caring.

It's now been more than eight years since that Monday afternoon when we got into the borrowed van still standing in our driveway. I remember it all so vividly. The back seats had been removed for the firewood Herb had brought home after helping his brother cut down a tree. Someone had emptied the wood, but our vehicles hadn't yet been exchanged. Besides, we needed the van to bring Andrew's things home from college. Mary and Chris brought rolled-up sleeping bags to sit on in the back. And there was Devona with her coat and sleeping bag!

Herb thought of how uncomfortable the ride would be and urged her not to come. I didn't want her to ride like that, either, but she insisted. It was not characteristic of Devona to push herself into a situation, but she just got into the back with Mary and Chris.

How did she know what we needed? Or did she know? It was clear to her that she had to be with us for this difficult journey. I felt secure having her along. Little did I know how much I would need her!

Highway 169 held excitement for us. In the eight years since we'd left St. Peter, we had traveled this highway many times. Especially Andrew. He had good friends in St. Peter, and, either by bus or by car, they often exchanged weekend visits. The only problem was that weekends were never long enough. And when he was ready for college, Gustavus Adolphus in St. Peter was his only choice. Just five weeks earlier on this same road and in this same van, we had taken Andrew off to college. On that recent day there had certainly been excitement. But I also remember some lumps in my stomach and some tears. Now, as we drove, we knew that only hours earlier, Andrew had taken his last ride over this road—a road that always held so much excitement for him. Today, it was hard to travel this road!

The funeral home was a landmark, as in many small towns, and we drove by it nearly every day when we lived there. It was next to the elementary schoolyard where Andrew had played, where one day in a sledding accident he had passed out. There had been a series of blackouts, and we, with his physician, had wondered if the accident happened because he had first passed out or if pain had caused him to check out. Careful neurological studies found no pathology. But there were moments after such episodes, looking out of our kitchen window to the mortuary below the hill, that I worried about Andrew. And now he was there!

I didn't want to go in. I didn't want it to be true. I remember feeling detached from the feet that walked my body through the door.

The funeral director on duty was our friend. Herb had been his pastor. I'd always admired his sensitive way of ministering to grievers while at the same time working so efficiently. Now it was our turn. There were things that had to be taken care of, but first he asked, "How are all of you doing?" When the right time came, he helped us make first one decision, then the next.

I was haunted by the fear of seeing what Andrew had done to his head, and whether we would be able to see him. It was all so unbelievable. We needed to see him dead to help us believe it. So did his friends. Could we have a viewing? I felt so relieved at last to get my question out and hear the answer, "Yes, there's no problem." But what would it be like to see Andrew in a coffin? Now we would have to choose one.

Bright lights. Coffins everywhere. Gray. Bronze. Wood. Blue and ivory satin. Our friend, the funeral director, was quoting prices and I heard nothing. Sights and sounds became one big blur. At last I turned my back to it all, in tears, sobbing with a rush of memories.

Beds. How I loved making my children's beds when they were babies, toddlers, little children. Even as they grew up, I still loved making up their beds with fresh sheets on wash day. Neighbor children used to ask, "Don't you have a dryer?" They wondered why our sheets were dried in the wind. "The bed smelled so fresh," our children would say in the morning. It was part of mother love. And now, a cold, sterile coffin for a bed?

Even though Herb, Mary, and Chris were right beside me, I suddenly felt so alone. Although grief may be shared, each of us approached it individually because of our own special relationship with Andrew. So, for each one in our family, the burden of loss was unique. Even two parents don't share the same feelings. Grief is very particular. That's why it's so lonely. You feel alone in the universe, as though the signposts are all gone. Directions have disappeared. You feel lost and scared and disoriented.

Devona stood with her arm around me as I got it out at last: "I don't want to buy a coffin!" How I needed her beside me! She, too, was a mother, and I felt her compassion. I felt her grief mingle with mine. She didn't say anything, and she didn't have to. Her very presence gave me stability; held me together when I was lost and disoriented. Thank you, Devona. Thanks for knowing you needed to be there.

12.
Comforting Soup

We needed to empty Andrew's dormitory room. His friends had offered to do it. So had their parents. But Mary and Chris had suddenly become very possessive. He was their brother, and they wanted no one else touching his things. College life was familiar to them. They needed to go to the dorm to be with his friends, to know everything his friends could tell them about Andrew, to pack his things carefully and lovingly. It was something they had to do. And they needed to do it together.

Before they went, Chris asked all of us to go to First Lutheran Church. On the way, we drove past the house we'd built and loved, and in the church we felt warmed with memories. We hugged each other and prayed and laughed and cried together. And then we walked out into the sunshine.

"It seems like no one should be driving today," said Chris, watching cars driving down the street. "Don't they know Andrew died?" That's how we all felt. If that sounds strange, it is strange. Grief is strange. When your world is shattered, nothing matters and one feels that nothing normal should go on in anyone else's life, either.

It was 2:30 when Chris unplugged Andrew's electric clock. It seemed to symbolize the stopping of his life. And in many ways, our clocks all stopped with his.

We went to the home of our good friend—the pastor who would be conducting the funeral—while Mary and Chris emptied

Andrew's room. We brought the funeral plans we had all worked out.

The aroma of homemade soup greeted us and filled the house. Our friends' house is cozy, and that day it seemed they had made it cozy just for us. I remember sinking down into the sofa, emotionally drained, and feeling cradled by it. Devona sat on one side and Herb on the other, while our friends surrounded us with their hospitality.

Hospitality, says Henri Nouwen, is providing space for strangers to tell where they've come from.[1] If one is helped to tell that story, says Nouwen, a wellspring within each of us will know which way to continue the journey. Grief needs such hospitality.

Our friends listened as we told our tragic journey of the past hours. It feels so good to be loved and listened to when you're wounded. When Mary and Chris returned, their stories joined with ours. Received with hospitality, we were all invited to their table.

I've always been fond of homemade soup. But never before or since has any soup tasted so good to me. Grief made me icy cold and felt like a hard ball in the pit of my stomach. For two days I hadn't eaten, and I was famished. Our friends had created a respite for us. When we told our story, the heavy ball of grief in my stomach was diminished, at least for a time. And the soup warmed us. God's presence quieted our stormy hearts, and it was symbolized by our friends' comforting soup.

Note

1. Henri J. M. Nouwen, *Reaching Out* (New York: Doubleday, 1975), 67–68.

13.
Charcoal Blazer

We were anxious to get home. But before leaving St. Peter, we had one more important errand. The visitation was to be the next day, and the funeral director needed Andrew's clothes.

Carefully Chris chose the newest and best: charcoal dress pants and a sharp charcoal blazer, still on the hanger from the store. Chris had laid them carefully on top of the load in the van.

It was fun helping Andrew pick out the blazer in a memorable shopping expedition just before school began. Andrew wanted Chris to go with us. We had a good time, the three of us. Dayton's department store had turned the air-conditioning way up that day, and I was cold. So, with a big grin, Andrew took off his khaki jacket covered with wisecrack buttons and draped it over me. I must have been a sight walking all over the store with that jacket on. Gray hair and all. At least those two big guys got lots of laughs. All I cared about was being warm! We decided on the charcoal flannel slacks and matching blazer—Andrew's first choice. Also a new white shirt and a tie. He looked great, and he knew it.

Herb stopped the van beside the funeral home. The sun hung low in the western sky, and cast long shadows. Chris stepped out of the van, lifting the hanger, heavy with memories and hopes. As we watched him walk into the shadow of the funeral home, his twenty-two years suddenly seemed to double. He came back empty-handed.

14.
Numb

I t was dark when we got home, and the house was full of people. More of our sisters had arrived—from California, South Carolina, and northern Minnesota. The looks on their faces were frightened and anguished. For they had loved Andrew, too. With each person who came to our house, the shared memories of Andrew flashed back.

Our family physician was there with his wife. Just a few weeks ago he'd given Andrew his college physical. What he was unable to complete was Andrew's medical history. *Unknown—Adopted* was scrawled across those blanks. It was the best he—or we—could do. There was no cure for that illness—the illness of lost identity. Andrew grieved over it. And died of it. To him it felt like a black hole.

"I've never seen anyone in this world I look like," he would say. "I feel sometimes like I don't belong in this world. Maybe I'm part elf."

And we found his poem about going to ancestors of other worlds. For Andrew, it was a fatal illness. He went off to college with this diagnosis: *Unknown—Adopted.* Even his doctor couldn't help.

Two dear friends were there from our first parish, near the vacation home we'd enjoyed for twenty years. They'd driven four hours to be with us that evening. Good parents, they, too, had been tested—at times to the limit. We'd discovered long ago that the load is lighter when shared, and such sharing was the essence of our friendship. We'd been to the Dairy Queen together the last time Andrew was with us at the lake.

He had been in trouble and needed our help. The cabin was a good place to be. That week we spent together at the lake became a time of healing and hope. Our friends stood by, listening to our fears and concerns, thankful with us that things were looking up.

But a curious thing happened on the day Andrew left the lake to go home. On his way out of the kitchen he stopped to hug me. With tears in his eyes he said, "Thanks for the food, Mom." After he'd gone, I felt troubled and told Herb about it. Adults often thanked me for the food after a visit with us at the lake, but it wasn't like an eighteen year old to say that, and it wasn't like Andrew. He was never so formal.

Was he trying to fit the new mold of an adult? Or was it gratitude for a new lease on life after this week? What did he mean? I pondered it in my heart, as another mother did so long ago. Was it a kind of poetic symbolism? His mind often worked that way. Food. Everything you've done and been for me, Mom. Was he saying all of that in those five weighty words? Did he know when he spoke them that he'd never return to this place he loved? This place of family closeness; of fishing at sunset; of games and popcorn at night. Mounting butterflies. Catching bats and snakes and frogs. Casting for bass in the bay. Tenting with friends. Full moons. Sunshine and storms. Rainbows. Love. And food.

Our friends from the lake didn't say much, but they came with pain in their eyes. They needed to be with us and we with them. Just seeing them brought so many memories—and understanding. Thanks, good friends, for being close!

Those were the most concentrated thirty-six hours I had ever experienced—from Sunday morning until Monday night. We had been surrounded and lifted up by loved ones and friends. We had been helped in so many ways. But no one else could bear our feelings. Excruciating and extreme as they were, we had been open and honest in acknowledging them to ourselves and in letting them pour out as they came. At the end of this long day, with our house full of people, my overload button went on. I was numb.

I remember saying words but feeling nothing. No sadness, no helplessness, no longing. It was as though a fuse had blown; the lights had gone out. I wondered what I looked like. Never in my life had I been in such a state. Did they wonder why I didn't cry or seem sad? Was I expressionless? Did they think I was in control, or that I had such wonderful faith? I couldn't articulate a thing. It was frightening, and I wondered what was happening to me. I felt detached from my body, unable to care about anything. It was terrible!

I became a person I had never known in my fifty-three years of life. Every cell in my body felt restless and nervous. I got up from my chair and wandered about. I remember our sisters serving coffee and cookies. Everyone and everything became a blur. I was numb. Perhaps with sleep I'd recover.

15.
You Have to
Be Strong

A friend said it to Chris at the visitation. "You have to be strong for your parents."

Confused, Chris came to us later asking, "What did he mean?"

Thankful that he hadn't just carried it around inside, I responded, "I don't know what he meant, but the best way for you to be strong for me is to be honest with your feelings and get them all out right away. Even if it's in the middle of the night, come and wake us." He seemed relieved to have a handle on it.

It was 6:00 A.M. on the day of the funeral. Toward morning we had both fallen into a deep sleep. We were awakened by a quiet voice saying, "Can we talk?" Chris jumped into the bed and sat on a pillow between us, just as he used to do when he was small. It wasn't the ordinary behavior of a young man his age.

But grief isn't ordinary. At such moments you revert to being a child again, longing for security. It had happened to me the day before. My father had arrived with one of my sisters and her husband. Our family had gathered in the home of a friend—a brief respite from receiving people at the funeral home where we would go again after dinner. Here in our friend's living room, sat my eighty-five-year-old father, reaching out to me, saying, "Oh, dear Corinne!" I let him gather me into his lap like a little child, hugging me as we wept together. Grief isn't ordinary.

I recalled a similar day forty-five years earlier. My favorite kitten had been run over by a car. Although one of many on the farm, she was the special one. Dad rarely noticed feelings,

YOU HAVE TO BE STRONG

but when he came in for morning coffee, he seemed to sense my sorrow. Taking me by the hand, he led me to the living room. There he lifted me into his lap and just let me cry. I remembered listening to his steady breathing and feeling his arms tight around me. At last my tears were all spent and I felt relieved. Then he went to have his coffee.

And so, as the first rays of dawn broke on that difficult day, Chris sat on a pillow between us, filled to the brim with thoughts and feelings. They came tumbling out! We cried with him. Then he began to remember good times with Andrew. And funny times. Those weren't hard to recall, for Andrew had a natural sense of humor. Soon, some brotherly secrets began to come out, and all three of us were laughing. It felt so good! We had wondered if we'd ever laugh again, and already we were laughing. On the day of his funeral! It surprised us that we could laugh, but Andrew would have liked that.

"Did you guys wonder what ever happened to all that masking tape down on the basement workbench?" asked Chris. "You bought it to use when we painted the house and it never got used."

"Well, yes," Herb said. "I've looked for it. What *did* happen to it?"

We didn't allow parties at our house when we were away. We had always covered the bases, or so we thought. The youth worker at church was very dependable. Andrew liked having him stay when we were away. They sat up and had late-night talks. Andrew's friends liked him, too. These were often important conversations.

But during Andrew's senior year of high school it was Chris, then living back at home, who was the chaperon when we were away.

"I let Andrew have parties," he confessed. "But I knew from experience and I told him, 'Be sure *everything* is just like Mom left it because she gets suspicious if *anything* looks different! And whatever you do, don't let *anyone* into the living room!' So Andrew made a grillwork out of masking tape over the foyer

49

archway into the living room. It worked perfectly! Not a soul went in there."

"Andrew, you rascal!"

This was only the beginning of many special times when we shared deep feelings with Chris and Mary. Back at the University of Wisconsin, Chris wrote: "I feel like someone who has had a limb cut off but still gets sensations from the limb that used to be there. . . . I've still got a lot of phantom pain, but I understand that it will eventually disappear. I don't think it ever will, but it's something I must live with."

Back in Arizona, Mary wrote: "I struggle with the pain every day and I'm trying to adjust myself to the fact that it is a hurt I (and you) will have to live with the rest of our lives. It is so hard—words seem so inept. I feel tired and at times wonder what the point is. Questions, with no answers, boggle my mind and confuse me until I become so frustrated, lost, and depressed. . . . My wish is that *hope* from the Divine Protector can brighten our days and that love may warm the empty cold spot we all feel aching deep in our hearts. I love you both so much."

It was hard for Chris to study those first weeks back at school. He called often. It was time for exams. "I can't concentrate. I can't possibly take my econ test. What will I do?" He had good friends, but they didn't understand grief. Fortunately, he had an uncle and aunt who understood and could intervene. He learned to use those who understood and who could listen. After driving home, he burst in the front door, sobbing. "It's so hard coming home the first time knowing Andrew's not here!"

Chris, neither you nor I knew what our friend meant that day at the visitation. But you and Mary have learned to express your feelings all along the way. By so doing, you have been strong for us. And because you've done that for yourselves, you've been able to help us by listening to our feelings. You've learned early in life the wisdom of Paul, "For whenever I am weak, then I am strong" (2 Cor. 12:10). You *have* been strong for us.

16.
Saying Good-bye

One has to say good-bye. We each do it in our own special way. I had said that to Mike, one of Andrew's closest friends. We wanted him and Andrew's other friends at the reviewal. Perhaps that would be a time when they could say their good-byes. So, first thing the next morning, Mike was at the front door asking me, "Where's Andrew's football jersey?"

"It's in his room somewhere," I said. "Why don't you go up and look for it? I think you know his room better than I!" In a few minutes he came bounding down the stairs, green and white school colors in hand.

What would it be like to go to the funeral home today? I didn't want to go, but at the same time, we were all so anxious to see Andrew! But to see him dead—how could I? I thought of the telephone call from the hospital two years earlier telling us that Andrew had been brought in by ambulance, unconscious from a car accident. A head injury. How frantic we had been to get there. How thankful when we reached the emergency room to find him awake. We had cried for joy. If only it could be that way again. But this was different.

There on the placard above the door: *Andrew Chilstrom*. Names, names, names. Yesterday it was *Andrew Chilstrom* on the obituary page. Today, outside his room at the funeral home. Other names, perhaps, but please, not Andrew's!

Mary needed to buy a long-stemmed rose and lay it beside him. It was her way of saying good-bye.

The funeral home was packed. The line was long. Over and over people said, "I don't know what to say!"

"You don't have to say anything," Herb said repeatedly, "just being here with us is what we need!"

Can anyone know how much his or her presence means in such a crisis? Words are barely heard and soon forgotten. But the *presence* of friends—bringing their love and sorrow, listening to ours. The memory of their coming—their faces, their tears, their embrace—is etched in our minds forever. Remembering is such a gift. As the months turn into years, remembering does bring back deep sorrow, but it also recalls for us that *presence when we needed it most.* It continues to be for us the *body of Christ.*

The line ended. Chairs were filled. High school and college friends were seated on the floor. It felt good to sit down in the quiet. Grief is exhausting. The pastor read scripture and led us in those seasoned prayers that are so helpful when we don't know what to say.

When the pastor was finished, Mike and some of his friends got up from the floor and surrounded the casket. Athletes. Handsome and eighteen years old. Football and wrestling buddies. They needed to do something to say good-bye. Lots of years they'd been together, and there they were, soul to soul, saying good-bye. You could have heard a pin drop. They began moving about and when they left there was a neatly folded green and white football jersey resting against his hand, "Number 1. Chilstrom." Later they told us they had also put a plug of chewing tobacco in his blazer pocket. No, we weren't happy that he and his friends had picked up that habit—a rite of passage, I suppose. But you have to say good-bye.

When we left for the funeral that morning, Chris scrambled for a pen. He wrote a note to put in his brother's pocket. We each had our own way of saying good-bye.

Hundreds came. The college chapel filled. As people came streaming in, I kept breaking back through the line to see Andrew one more time—that beautiful child I'd cradled and loved since he was nine days old. I grieved also for another mother who had cradled him in her womb for nine months. The unknown mother

I'd prayed for these eighteen years, the one who didn't know her son was dead.

A few days after the funeral Herb sent our letter to Lutheran Social Services of New Jersey, the agency through which we had adopted Andrew. "It is with a sense of deep regret and intense grief that I share with you the news that our adopted son, Andrew, died on Sunday, November 11, 1984. . . . I have no idea, of course, whether Andrew's birth mother will ever make a search for him. In the event she does, we want to make certain that this information is in his file. We also would want her to know that we would be very open—in fact, anxious—to meet her, share with her everything she wants to know about her remarkable son, and acquaint her with the places that were familiar to him as he grew from childhood to young adulthood."

The agency sent a sympathetic response, confirming our understanding of the feelings of a birth mother. We were "moved by your sensitivity to Andrew's birth mother and your willingness to share your memories and knowledge of him with her. We know from our experience that birth mothers do not forget their children, and indeed mourn for their loss, though without the knowledge of the kind of person their baby became."

I reached out to touch Andrew's chest, putting my hand over his heart. His tender heart. His broken heart. The body, always so supple and responsive, now felt hard like cement. I used to cup his head in my hands and smell the sunshine. I expected some day to welcome his little children as they came in from outdoors, and smell the sunshine again. I put my head down to touch his and sobbed, oblivious to the mourners going by.

It was time for the service to begin. The casket had been closed. Someone came to say, "Don just came and never saw Andrew." Don was the last person Andrew had talked with. A special friend. Of all people, Don must say good-bye. I went with him to the funeral director. He opened the casket while we stood there. Don had to say good-bye.

The funeral was a time to grieve. It was also a time to hear God's word of promise. And never had I heard the words from

Romans 8 as I did that day. The Spirit burned them into my heart!

> If God is for us, who is against us? He who did not withhold his own Son, but gave him up for all of us, will he not with him also give us everything else? . . . It is God who justifies. Who is to condemn? It is Christ Jesus, who died, yes, who was raised, who is at the right hand of God, who indeed intercedes for us. Who will separate us from the love of Christ? Will hardship, or distress, or persecution, or famine, or nakedness, or peril, or sword? . . . No, in all these things we are more than conquerors through him who loved us. For I am convinced that neither death, nor life, nor angels, nor rulers, nor things present, nor things to come, nor powers, nor height, nor depth, nor anything else in all creation, will be able to separate us from the love of God in Christ Jesus our Lord (Rom. 8:31-39).

I was sure for Andrew. And for me.

As I followed the coffin down the aisle, I couldn't look up. My mind was riveted on him. My hand was on his casket, and I longed to touch him. Then we took the long slow journey to his grave.

After the pastor had read scripture, Herb moved slowly to the head of Andrew's coffin. Every day for eighteen years he had prayed for Andrew. A broken father, he would now release him back to God. His words were sorrowful and pleading:

> Into your hands, O merciful Savior, we commend your servant, *Andrew*. Acknowledge, we humbly beseech you, a sheep of your own fold, a lamb of your own flock, a sinner of your own redeeming. Receive him into the arms of your mercy, into the blessed rest of everlasting peace, and into the glorious company of the saints in light (*LBW*, 211).

Everyone was silent as Andrew was lowered into the earth. I peeled off a petal of the rose I held. It floated down with him. Another petal. Another. And another. Until the petals were all gone. Like his life.

We each had to say our own good-bye.

17.
Rituals Are
Important

Visitation. Funeral service. Graveside committal. Lunch at the church. These rituals are necessary. The community gathers to acknowledge that one has died, never to be among us again, and to tell mourners, I know this has happened to you and I'm here for you in this time of crisis. I'm here to mourn with you and to hear the gospel, God's good news; to stand beside you with hope and promise, walking with you as you reenter your world of reality. (See appendix for the funeral sermon preached by the Rev. Dennis J. Johnson.)

Lunch at the church. How many times I had brought fresh cakes or hot dishes for a funeral. But it wasn't until *this* day that I knew how important this ritual really was! Important because after these strenuous days of shock, the focus began to turn from the one lost to the task of living without him. Our community was there in full force to support us on our grief journey.

As I followed his coffin down the aisle, I couldn't free myself from total thoughts of Andrew. Though gregarious by nature, I couldn't lift my eyes. I didn't know who had come. Only one face did I see, as we paused by the door. It was the man who had been Andrew's counselor. At the graveside, many spoke to us before having to leave. Over lunch at the church, folks lingered.

One by one they came, as soon as we sat down. The interruptions didn't matter because we couldn't eat anyway. Each came, forming a link for us with our future—a future forever changed because we no longer had this precious son.

55

A major grief is truly a root experience, for one is cut off, as it were, at the root. One survives. But the new plant will be different. Feeling vulnerable, like with an open wound, we were grateful to be surrounded with love. It was protection against the wound. It was assurance that caring people would be there for us during our metamorphosis, while we learned to walk again.

Family and friends had come, some traveling great distances. Andrew's cousins had left school and work to be with us. Their young, warm love was so comforting! Like Andrew's friends, they seemed frightened and needed our love, too. It was a mutual sharing, but for us their young hugs were a special kind of comfort.

One cousin couldn't come. He was on his adventure, traveling abroad. But he had had a dream, knowing somehow that there was pain. And, though he did not know why, his thoughts and prayers were with us on that day. Later came his thoughtful, sensitive letter.

The first wave of terrible shock had passed. Having our community with us in God's presence, helping us give Andrew back to God and bury his precious body bonded us to them. We felt more peaceful now, lingering over lunch, more open to receive comfort. Folks were saying good-bye and heading home. But they had solidified their presence, which would continue to be with us even across the miles.

Each had a special way of standing by. Some called Saturday mornings, at first every week. Others wrote often. Some sent flowers on the anniversary of Andrew's death and on his birthday. Some continue to write on those important days, knowing we weep again.

There were the friends who first took us to meet Mary and Chris at the airport. In their back seat we sat together with our children, so close and yet so alone as the sinking sun filled the sky with red. Our friends felt with us that night. And still, every November they write, remembering Andrew and aware that our sorrow continues.

The retired pastor, neither relative nor close friend, unassuming but ever sensitive, had been at all the rituals. Somehow, because of his own life experience, he knew the importance of standing by, upholding those who grieve. His notes came often at first, then further apart. Sometimes there was just a postcard with a simple message: "Just want you to know I'm thinking of you today and praying for you." On the anniversary of Andrew's death he sent another message, signed simply with his initials. Now, years later, his notes are less frequent, but still they come. He'll never know what those little notes have meant to us. From him I've learned to do the same. The gift of comfort received is an investment; comfort to share with others. From God and from the Body of Christ. "Blessed be the God and Father of our Lord Jesus Christ, the Father of mercies and the God of all consolation, who consoles us in all our affliction, so that we may be able to console those who are in any affliction with the consolation with which we ourselves are consoled by God" (2 Cor. 1:3-4).

18.
Failure

There was only one face that I remember seeing as our family walked with Andrew's coffin out of the chapel. Full of tears, it was the face of Andrew's counselor.

When Andrew's growing anger became obvious, we went to him. He was a fine counselor—one of the best. Andrew liked him. He was sensitive, perceptive, and wise. But Andrew didn't cooperate. Nor did he seek out a counselor at college as he'd promised. Nevertheless, he was afraid of his own anger.

Andrew was angry at adoption. Though he was close to us, his adoptive family, he needed to know and claim his birth family. In school, family tree assignments upset him. In ninth grade, he came home one day, slammed down his books, and said, "Mom, do you realize I'll have the name Chilstrom my whole life?" Then he shouted, "And I am German!"

More and more he noticed likenesses within families of his friends and would repeat, "I don't look like anyone I've ever seen. Sometimes I feel like I don't belong in this world." We were grateful that he felt free to express his pain, but it hurt.

In their research on adoption, David Brodinsky and Marshall Schecter write of

> opposing irreconcilable dilemmas: on the advice traditionally given the parents (he) is told early in (his) life that (he) comes from a different family of origin. (He) comes to learn, but not understand, that the mother of whom (he) was once a part has been inextricably lost. . . . Is there some yet-unexplained inner force

compelling them to find someone who looks like them, feels like them, laughs like them, is artistic like them—a need to fill a void or give them a sense of completeness with a full familiar history? . . . For the adoptee the missing experience of perceiving likeness-to-self is compounded by the lack of a full and coherent birth story. . . . Since the need for cognitive understanding of causal relationships is inherent in the human (Piaget, 1954 [Brodinsky's reference]) limitations and discrepancies in birth information result both in a plethora of fantasies, none or few supported by reality, and in cognitive dissonances that demand reconciliation. . . . For some adopted persons the absence of a sense of human connectedness assumes intolerable proportions at a conscious level.[1]

Betty Jean Lifton, herself an adopted person, discusses this absence of human connectedness in her book, *Lost and Found.* It is important to this author that those who had no experience understand what it's like growing up adopted.

In the late 1930s we have the psychiatrist Florence Clothier speaking out like a modern-day Cassandra:

The child who does not grow up with his own biological parents, who does not even know them or anyone of his own blood, is an individual who has lost the thread of family continuity. A deep identification with our forebears, as experienced originally in the mother-child relationship, gives us our most fundamental security. Every adopted child, at some point in his development, has been deprived of this primitive mother. This trauma and the severing of the individual from his racial antecedents lie at the core of what is peculiar to the psychology of the adopted child.

Lifton, speaking from her personal experience, writes,

Sometimes when I'm with nonadopted friends, I will spring the question, "Did you ever think you weren't born?" I get quizzical looks as to my seriousness or sanity, but always the reply, "Of course, I was born." For without knowing it, while they were growing up, they heard random fragments about how they kicked in the womb, how Mama almost didn't make it to the hospital, and without understanding it, they were receiving direct confirmation about their entrance into the universe and their place in the flow of the generations. But the adoptee says: "I'm not sure I ever was born." Because the womb is a forbidden, lost place, the condition of having been born becomes lost to him too. Without the original birth certificate, he has no proof.[2]

Edwin Shneidman carries further the discussion of Brodinsky and Schecter's "opposing irreconcilable dilemmas" and their consequent "intolerable proportions" in his book *Definition of Suicide:*

> Ageneratic suicides are those in which the self-inflicted death relates primarily to the individual's "falling out" of the procession of generations; his losing (or abrogating) his sense of membership in the march of generations and, in this sense, in the human race itself. . . .

> This sense of belonging and place in the scheme of things, especially in the march of generations, is not only an aspect of middle and old age, but it is a comfort and a characteristic of psychological maturity, at whatever age. To have no sense of serial belonging or to be an "isolate" is truly a lonely and comfortless position, for then one may, in that perspective, truly have nothing to live for. This kind of hermit is estranged not only from his contemporaries but, much more importantly, he is alienated from his ancestors and his (fellow) descendants, from his inheritance and his bequests. He is without a sense of the majestic flow of the generations: He is ageneratic.[3]

Some seem to handle adoption well, but for others the incongruence is overwhelming. They have an amended birth certificate saying they were born to adoptive parents, but are told there is another set of parents society calls "natural." That creates conflict. They are told they may not have their original birth certificate. That creates conflict. They're assigned a family tree. More conflict. The physician asks for medical history when they have none. Conflict. "You're chosen and special," they're told.

But the other side of the coin is that someone gave them up. When asked, we tell them, "Your birth mother gave you up because she loved you." And deep inside they wonder Why? and live with the nagging feeling of being unwanted. Conflict.

Someday, Andrew said, he wanted a family. "Do you realize, when my first child is born, it will be the first time in my life I'll see someone who looks like me?" He longed for that day, and yet dreaded passing on a missing genetic link to his children. Meanwhile, lots of girlfriends. So much conflict. And tenderness. His tenderness came out in a poem he wrote many months earlier before the darker clouds gathered.

Home
I want a small house with a white picket fence
    and a gate that needs oiling.
I want a great big yard and a hammock in the shade
    and a dog that chases butterflies.
I want a loving wife with a sweet smile
    and an apron that says "Mom."
But most of all, I want you, God,
    To be there in my house
Watching over my wife, my children,
    My hammock in the shade,
    And my dog that chases butterflies.

Days later, his counselor came out to our home. He couldn't help Andrew and felt failure.

The youth director at our church had spent many hours with Andrew. In the end, he couldn't help him, and he felt failure.

The resident assistant in Andrew's section of the college dorm spent a great deal of time with him. Unaware of how critical these missing pieces were becoming for Andrew, he couldn't help and felt failure.

Each of us—parents, brother, sister—were always there for him, but it wasn't enough. And we all felt failure.

His counselor's face is the only one I remember. The face with streaming tears mirrored us all. We'd all given our best and failed. We felt failure, but not blame.

61

Notes

1. David M. Brodinsky and Marshall D. Schecter, *The Psychology of Adoption* (New York: Oxford University Press, 1990), 63–65.

2. Betty Jean Lifton, *Lost and Found* (New York: Harper & Row, 1988), 20.

3. Edwin Shneidman, *Definition of Suicide* (New York: John Wiley & Sons, 1985), 26.

19.
You Can't Keep
Grief Inside

Even in those first frightening moments, shaking and in a state of shock, we wanted to hide the truth. Andrew had died by his own hand, and we were stunned with grief that he was dead. But compounding that grief was the fact that he had died by suicide.

Furthermore, we were public people. Herb was the bishop of three hundred thirty Lutheran churches in the state of Minnesota. Publicity, news media, misunderstandings—how could we face all that? The prospect was overwhelming! "Can't we hide it?" we asked ourselves as we sat trembling in our family room that morning. At that moment, no one knew.

But we didn't wonder long. Herb and I both knew what happens when you conceal or avoid deep grief. Sadness becomes crusted over with anger. It's destructive and creates barriers with those you love most. You dump it on those around you. We had seen the devastating consequences of anger projected onto others. We knew better than to keep such an enormous grief hidden.

Repressing suffering "becomes a way of life," says Douglas John Hall, "and there are vast areas of experience upon which we dare not reflect consciously even for a moment . . . it becomes the greatest threat both to our sanity and to our survival.

"Consequences of the repression of suffering are devastating . . . even . . . dangerous." He lists three consequences: (1) difficulty in accepting or articulating one's own personal suffering; (2) inability to enter imaginatively into the suffering of others; (3) searching for the enemy (unconsciously, of course).[1]

Sadness turns to anger a layer at a time. Think of an onion. Once you peel off the outer layer of inexplicable anger, you find other layers beneath. And when you peel back many layers of anger (peeling away anger smarts for those standing by, just like peeling an onion), at last you get to the inner core, which is sadness. Deep inside is a very tender sadness. Sometimes the sadness is buried with tears never shed, locked up for many years. I've seen men weep as they ask, Why am I crying? That happened forty years ago.

But unexpressed grief does not just disappear, as J. R. Hodge explains. "If the grief work is not actively pursued, the process may be fixated, aborted, or delayed. . . . However, almost certainly a distorted form of grief work will appear at some time in the future."[2] Avoiding grief is the American way. We want to avoid the painful emotions necessary to grieve. The consequence is pathological grief, an inability to terminate the process.

Conversely, Hodge describes normal grief as a "reintegration process which includes awareness of the loss combined with both physical and emotional effects drawn together into healing."[3]

"We, as a culture, have done a disservice to ourselves and to our loved ones," Cantor says, "by rewarding the ability to control disruptive emotion with great admiration. We have managed to cripple the work of mourning. . . . By minimizing the feelings and rituals of bereavement we have undermined an essential mode of healing.

"Intense grief is an unwelcomed experience; it can evoke strong feelings of helplessness, fear, guilt, and defeat. It is not surprising that we attempt to minimize it. Bereavement is not an easy or speedy task. In fact, it takes far more courage and strength to be open to the work of mourning, to be willing to experience one's vulnerability, actually to walk among the sufferers, than it does to erect a fortress of emotional armor around one's heart and remain forever hidden behind its protective barricades. . . . The painful work of mourning (is) essential to the preservation of rich and meaningful existence. The unmourned loss can haunt one's life and cause an experience of inexplicably bitter sadness. Anything lost must be accepted and mourned before it is possible to honor a loved memory and begin a new chapter of life. The process of grief can replenish each of us if we will but entrust ourselves to its healing powers."[4]

"No," Herb and I concluded. "We can't hide it!" The decision was quick and certain. We were both sure. We'll be open and forthright. We'll tell our story, however painful. Just maybe, in our truthfulness, we can help someone else. We knew it was the only way.

The question lasted only as long as it took to ask. The words came strong from deep within our souls. We both knew, *You can't keep grief inside.* It's the only road to healing.

Notes

1. Douglas John Hall, *God and Human Suffering* (Minneapolis: Augsburg, 1986), 43–46.

2. J. R. Hodge, "They that Mourn," *Journal of Religion and Health* 2 (1972): 229.

3. Hodge, "They that Mourn," 230.

4. Robert Chernin Cantor, *And a Time to Live* (New York: Harper & Row, 1978), 54–55.

20.
Sadness at Funerals

Many believe that if we have hope for everlasting life, we should make funerals a time of rejoicing. Hope of everlasting life is reason for rejoicing. But there is also a time for mourning, and we must be allowed sadness at funerals. Especially when death is untimely and unexpected.

Paul Romstad sees a growing trend to make funerals a celebration. Hymns in our *Lutheran Book of Worship* are the yardstick. He finds a decreasing number of funeral hymns in each successive book of worship—eleven in the 1913 edition; seven in the 1958 edition; and none in the 1978 edition. We might also note that lament psalms have been excluded entirely from this most recent worship resource.

When my father died at the age of ninety-one, he had lived a long and fruitful life. It was truly a time of celebration for his "homegoing." When our son died suddenly and unexpectedly in his eighteenth year, it was a tragedy. We could not make his funeral a celebration.

Martin Luther, when his thirteen-year-old daughter Magdalena died, wrote, "I am joyful in spirit but I am sad according to the flesh. The flesh doesn't take kindly to this. The separation [caused by death] troubles me above measure. It's strange to know that she is surely at peace and that she is well off there, very well off, and yet to grieve so much!"[1]

Calling for a return to sadness at funerals, Romstad suggests that this is a time for grieving. "If we're not ready to acknowledge the darkness we feel in the hymns and Scriptures at the funeral, how can the light of Christian hope break in?"[2]

Ecclesiastes 3:4 says there is "a time to weep." Romstad helps us when he says, "If the Gospel is to heal us, we can't keep hiding our grief under a bushel."[3] It is fitting to allow sadness at funerals.

Notes

1. Martin Luther, *Table Talk*, vol. 54 of *Luther's Works* (Philadelphia: Fortress Press, 1967), 432.

2. Paul O. Romstad, "Funerals," *Lutheran Standard* (March 1986): 16.

3. Romstad, "Funerals," 16.

21.
Shock

I t was the day after Andrew's funeral. People had departed, and our house had grown quiet. My sister and her daughter were still there. We needed milk, and my niece, Tami, said, "I'll take you to the store."

I remember walking around the kitchen that morning with salt and pepper shakers in my hand, not knowing what to do with them. It's a terrible feeling to be in shock.

I decided it would be good to go to a grocery store again. Tami and I walked in, picked up a carton of milk, and went to the cashier. "That will be two dollars and eight cents," he said. I fumbled in my billfold. Nothing made sense. I pulled at some bills and struggled with coins. I felt so uncoordinated. He must have wondered about me. Tami stood watching. Several minutes, and at last I conquered it. I gave the cashier two dollar bills and eight cents. I felt embarrassed.

As we got into the car, I started crying. "Tami, did you see what a terrible time I had figuring out change?"

"Yes," she replied, "but you did it!"

Two days later, on a Saturday morning, we had the neighbors in for morning coffee. We didn't know them very well, so we wondered, What was it like for them, having someone die by suicide next door? Was it scary? How did they feel? We invited them in to talk. Twelve came.

We told the whole story. They'd seen the commotion, the police cars, the coroner. They wanted to listen, and they had their own stories to tell. It was good to connect, but it was also wrenching.

When they were gone, I needed to go to the pharmacy. Without realizing that I hadn't driven my car since Andrew's death six days earlier, I just took off. Suddenly I heard a siren and saw a flashing light behind me. I pulled over and an officer came to my window. I looked up. It was the same officer who had come when we called so frantically six days ago! "Do you know what the speed limit is here?" he asked me.

"Forty," I replied.

"You were going fifty." As he spoke, he saw the tears in my eyes. "Is something wrong?"

Such a coincidence! "Yes," I said, "we've just had the neighbors in to talk about our tragedy and I'm reliving last Sunday when you came to our house." By now the tears were streaming down my cheeks.

He looked at me. "I don't think you should be driving."

"I shouldn't. But I didn't realize it when I got into my car."

Again I saw the kindness in his face as he replied, "I don't have any tickets with me. Go ahead, but be careful."

Driving is dangerous when we're in shock or grief. It is important to ask for help.

22.
Communion of Saints

No words can describe how we are lifted and carried by the communion of saints during such a crisis. Nor can words describe what the communion of saints is. But it is real—a powerful experience—and we are forever grateful. What it meant for us is best described through vignettes from the letters that poured in.

> You must know that very many people are thinking of you and interceding for you during these difficult days. There is little that any of us can say to ease the pain you feel, but perhaps it helps a little to know that many stand beside you in the community of grief. . . . [We] are among them. God will enfold you in the strong and gracious arms of his steadfast love.

> We want you to know we are hurting for you. . . . Words seem so empty. . . . All we can say is that we care and are pouring out our hearts in prayer for you.

> [We] join the many others who want to reach out to you in this time of terrible grief and loss. . . . You know you are truly surrounded by a great cloud of witnesses who love and support you. Please consider us among them.

> My heart aches for you! There are no words adequate to express the amount of love, sympathy, and feelings that stir inside those of us who love you. . . . I feel I knew your son so well, because

once in a while in years past you shared a bit of his struggle. Your love for him always showed so vividly.

From friends whose illness kept them from being with us:

We, too, felt the pain and anguish of Andrew's death. It makes us aware that life is always a struggle from birth to death. There is no peace except the kind that comes with living with the struggle and trusting, when trusting seems futile, in God's grace and mercy. . . . [We] listened to the tape of the funeral service. It was for us a service of real transcendence—the words of Scripture, the words of . . . [the] sermon helped us to feel a part of the church that has preached hope and salvation through its long history and that we live with the saints beyond and the saints present. I hope you, too, were lifted up knowing we were all there with you.

Although we have been spared the rending experience which you and your loved ones have undergone, we nevertheless know that the reality of the communion of saints often becomes vivid in the midst of catastrophic circumstance. As fellow members of that communion, we want you to know that our prayers join with others on your behalf. God bless and keep you and yours to the glory of our Lord Jesus Christ.

Many friends stand with you giving support . . . in your grief. We, too, want to be numbered among them. . . . We assure you of our inner communion with you in our thoughts and prayers for you and with you. We believe with you that Christ is present even in the darkness that accompanies such a personal loss as that of Andrew, much loved son and brother. God be with you.

And from a letter quoting J. S. Bach's Passion According to St. Matthew:

My heart is so full that there aren't words—only that I love you I love you I love you! "When life begins to fail me, I fear not having Thee. When pains of death assail me, My comfort Thou wilt be. Whene'er from woes that grieve me I seek to find relief, Alone thou wilt not leave me, for thou hast tasted grief."

71

23.
A Party

We were concerned about Andrew's friends. We were grieving, but so were they. They were used to calling often. And they came often to our house. They each used to grab a cap off the hooks going down to the basement family room when they gathered to play penny poker. They'd been there for a big salmon feed on Andrew's eighteenth birthday. They'd been there for parties we knew about and some that we didn't.

Thanksgiving was coming. Andrew's classmates would be home from college. It would seem strange for them not to come to Andrew's house, so we decided to have a party. "Spread the word," we told his two closest friends. "Everyone's welcome. Come from seven to eleven on Friday evening." We filled the refrigerator with pop and pizzas, and wondered who would come!

The party had been our impetus for cleaning out Andrew's room. It was hard boxing up his clothes, but with our minds on the approaching party, we rushed purposefully into the task. We sorted out the T-shirts and jackets Chris and Mary wanted, and gave the rest away. We dismantled the heavily laden bulletin board. Ski trip stickers. Banners. Posters. Doonesbury comic strips. They all went into a big wide box on the landing by the front door. Julie and Andrew's best friends would get first pick.

Seven o'clock. They began to arrive—friends from high school, church, and those in college home for Thanksgiving. Forty kids came. They loved being back in Andrew's house. They needed to be there, to be with us. We cried together and laughed. Told stories, shared memories. We hugged, drank pop, ate pizza. We shared our love for Andrew, and our sorrow, missing him.

All evening it felt as though he would show up any minute. He was always there when any of these kids were around. Maybe that's why when eleven o'clock came, they seemed reluctant to leave. They hadn't seen Andrew yet. But that was the point of their coming together in our home. To realize in the shock and confusion of grief that Andrew really was gone; that he would not be back.

When the last one had gone it seemed so quiet. So sad. But we felt good, too. For we had helped them grieve. And they had helped us. It was new healing for us all. And the box on the landing, heaped with Andrew's mementos when they arrived, was empty.

24.
Christmas Card

Of the many condolence cards that arrived, some we knew we needed to read again. And again. And again. I began to put them into a cake pan so we'd know exactly where they would be when needed. For example, one card contained these lines from J. R. Miller:

> The happiest, sweetest, tenderest homes are not those where there has been no sorrow, but those which have been overshadowed with grief, and where Christ's comfort was accepted. The very memory of the sorrow is a gentle benediction that broods ever over the household, like the silence that comes after prayer. There is a blessing sent from God in every burden of sorrow.

It was painful to send out a Christmas card without Andrew's name. And then one of his friends sent a card Andrew had made at a youth retreat. His benediction. His signature. It was just right. We used it with the lines above for our 1984 Christmas card.

25.
Condolences Are
Important

I've sent many condolences. But I never fully realized how important they are. Each day they arrived—a new stack. Phone calls. Flowers. Letters and cards—a bushel full.

In shock those first days, we couldn't respond. Others opened envelopes for us, organized memorial gifts, recorded everything. Bit by bit, as we were able, we began to read the messages. Family, friends, business acquaintances, all acknowledging that Andrew had died. They sorrowed with us and felt our grief. They needed to tell us.

Each message was a gift. A bridge over the chasm in our life. We needed to know that these people, important in our world, knew of our abyss. Each message was a link in the chain that would lift us out of the pit and back onto the path of our lives. Sudden and extreme grief feels like a cutting off from life. So each message was important, also, because we were reconnected to those who sent it.

We had read dozens and dozens of cards and letters. No one had kept track of who had written. But some weeks after Andrew's death I said to Herb, "There are four people we haven't heard from." And he replied, "Yes, there are four," and named them. The same four I'd been thinking of! We'd been reconnected to all the other important people in our lives except these four. We felt estranged.

Did they know that Andrew had died? Did they care? What should we do when we saw them next? Tell them? Avoid them?

How could we have any conversation without bridging this enormous gap? By not acknowledging Andrew's death they had alienated themselves from us. We didn't know what to do.

For fourteen months it stayed that way. Then, on January 26, Andrew's birthday, I did something for Andrew and for us. I wrote to all four saying we had never heard from them when Andrew died. That perhaps they hadn't known what to say. That we didn't know how to relate to them without first talking about this together. That they were important to us. If they could write to us and say anything, in any way they were able, it would help us. "Please," I wrote to them, "please do this, if you can."

Shortly after receiving my letter, one of the four came to town on business. He said he'd gotten my letter. He explained his feelings of sadness when he had heard the news. Many times he had tried to write and nothing had seemed right. Weeks and months had gone by and then it had seemed too late. He expressed deep feelings. He bridged the gap. And we felt closer than ever to him and his whole family.

Another wrote, saying he never knew how much he dared to express. His letter was like a journaling. Once he began, the feelings flowed freely. Deeply sensitive. I'd given him permission to be close.

The other two never wrote. One never discussed the letter. Some years later we were at the baptism of her child, a very moving time for this young mother. We embraced, and she wept. She did answer my letter, but not with words. And we are close.

The fourth person has never mentioned the letter. I don't think she's able to do so. For many years now it has been awkward to be around her. At first I needed to avoid her. But gradually it began to feel safe. Slowly she is answering, but not with words.

26.
Words of Healing

Grief is chaotic and it dries up the words of prayer. In the long journey of grief, how does one pray when there are often no words? Sometimes when words did come, I found my thoughts going in circles, endless circles. I felt like I was sinking and, finally stuck.

Daniel Simundson's book, *Where Is God in My Suffering?* helped me to pray using lament psalms, "a prayer for times like that. . . . Laments allow honesty, realism, and integrity . . . keep the conversation with God open . . . help break down our isolation in times of suffering. . . . A lament helps us work through a process that is often necessary in times of suffering. A typical lament begins with a complaint addressed to God. It is important that it is addressed to God. It is not just a purposeless whining into the wind, but it is a coming to God, the one who can help . . . but ends with praise. The one crying out of the depths has been heard and concludes the psalm with praise of God who saves."[1]

In my sadness, I stood like a timid, fearful child, waiting at God's door, when the lament psalm, words from God, as it were, opened the door leading me to wholeness. The goal of the lament psalm is to cast our agony on God. This requires trust. That is very difficult, for the human spirit insists it can handle grief. It comes neither naturally nor easily to allow God to carry our burden.

There is significant movement in the lament psalm. Its very structure draws the griever into a process that lifts us out of the place where we were stuck in self-pity, moving us toward wholeness, out of lament into trust and praise.

Claus Westermann opens to us the action inherent within the lament psalm structure which brings movement to our grieving by showing us its various parts.

Address "is something like opening a door. . . . Contact is established which makes speaking with God possible. . . . If a person calls upon God by his name . . . something happens at that moment. The address is an event which unites the one who calls with the one who is called."[2] Even calling out God's name begins to lift us out of ourself. "Hear my prayer, O Lord, let my cry come to you (Ps. 102:1).

Complaint helps us cry out our sorrow. "Once we have had the opportunity to say our piece, then we will be better able to hear the good news that God has heard our pleas and will come to help."[3]

Do not hide your face from me
    in the day of my distress,
Incline your ear to me;
    answer me speedily in the day when I call.
For my days pass away like smoke,
    and my bones burn like a furnace.
My heart is stricken and withered like grass;
    I am too wasted to eat my bread.
Because of my loud groaning
    my bones cling to my skin.
I am like an owl of the wilderness,
    like a little owl of the waste places.
I lie awake;
    I am like a lonely bird on the housetop.
All day long my enemies taunt me;
    those who deride me use my name for a curse.
For I eat ashes like bread,
    and mingle tears with my drink,
because of your indignation and anger;
    for you have lifted me up and thrown me aside.

My days are like an evening shadow;
   I wither away like grass. . . .
"O my God," I say, "do not take me away
   at the mid-point of my life,
you whose years endure
   throughout all generations."
                  (Ps. 102:2-11, 24)

The complaint in a lament psalm helps us, first, to sort out our grief. We are helped to *own our suffering*, to pray with the psalmist, "I" and "we" (see also Lam. 5). It is *our suffering* and we must own it in the presence of God.

Second, *we're given permission and even help to lash out at God!* "You have lifted me up and thrown me aside" (102:10). Anger at God must be owned and spent in God's presence. We have to be open with our deepest feelings to be healed. Jesus used a lament psalm (22:1) on the cross when he cried out, "My God, my God, why have you forsaken me?" (Matt. 27:26). "Jesus was fully human. He knew what it was like to feel so alone and frightened that it was as if God had left. But Jesus is also God. And that means that God knows about our suffering. God has been there with us. When we cry out to God in our times of suffering, we know that we will be heard by one who truly knows what we have gone through. It is a great comfort for a sufferer to know the presence of an understanding and compassionate God, who not only invites our very human prayers but also knows what it is like to be in so much pain. God hears. God understands. God suffers with us. The lament is heard by one who has been there."[4]

Third, the complaint *helps us define the "enemies" and the destruction "they" bring.*

My heart is stricken and withered like grass;
   I am too wasted to eat my bread. . . .
I lie awake;
   I am like a lonely bird on the housetop.
All day long my *enemies* taunt me (Ps. 102:4, 7, 8; see also Pss.
   13 and 23).

79

I become aware as I pray, *these are my enemies.* They are against my health. They will consume me! I must name them in God's presence. As I pray the words of the psalmist, I become aware of how destructive are the enemies and how urgently I need God's help to overcome them.

Review of God's past acts does two things. Although I am broken now, I sense again that God *was* in my history. But I realize anew that my total history is within God's acts. *It is God and only God who can heal my brokenness.*

> "But you, O Lord, are enthroned forever;
>   your name endures to all generations.
> You will rise up and have compassion on Zion,
>   for it is time to favor it;
>   the appointed time has come. . . .
> Long ago you laid the foundation of the earth,
>   and the heavens are the work of your hands"
>   (Ps. 102:12-13, 25). (See also Isa. 51:9-16 and 63:11-14;
>   Pss. 74:12-17, 85, 89, 106)

When the contrast between the past and present is placed before him, what becomes noticeable is the awakening of a sense of history. Under the pressure of the crisis this causes the persons involved to perceive two things. First, as they behold the contrast of the past and the present, they begin to see similar integrating coherences in their own history, even at the point of rupture which exposes the stark contrast they currently experience. Second, they become aware of the fact that the totality of their history rests in the acts of God alone, who heals the ruptures."[5]

Petition is the goal of the complaint. Using the psalmist's words, I dare ask for God's attention. "Hear my prayer. . . . Do not hide your face. . . . Incline your ear to me. . . . Answer me speedily. . . . Do not take me away at the mid-point of my life." I call now upon God to intervene, to heal, to bring me again to wholeness.

Divine response happens as I pray the psalm.

> For the Lord will build up Zion;
>   he will appear in his glory.

He will regard the prayer of the destitute,
and will not despise their prayer.
Let this be recorded for a generation to come,
so that a people yet unborn may praise the Lord:
that he looked down from his holy height,
from heaven the Lord looked at the earth,
to hear the groans of the prisoners,
to set free those who were doomed to die;
so that the name of the Lord may be declared in Zion,
and his praise in Jerusalem,
when peoples gather together,
and kingdoms, to worship the Lord (Ps. 102:16-18).

Vow to praise happens with the psalmist's words, and praise bursts forth!

It happens because the griever with the psalmist has
taken a step beyond the complaint. By a declaration of confidence
the psalmist has entered territory where the complaint can be
silenced. Powers which threaten to destroy the suppliant's life are
not the only powers that exist. There is one power in which the
psalmist can trust: "But I have trusted in thy steadfast love."
Attached to this declaration of trust reversing the complaint is a
promise that at the same time also forms the conclusion of the
psalm. . . . In the newly-won confidence based on God's goodness,
the petitioner—with daring faith—now has stepped forth into the
hour of deliverance, in which he will rejoice in God's help. . . .
The lamenters, in the brief space of prayer, stepped out of complaint into trust, into the certainty that their prayers had been
heard, into an anticipation of the jubilation experienced by those
who have been delivered. . . . More is at work than a "change
in mood" . . . we are dealing with a direct witness—the direct
reflection—of an intervention from outside, from beyond; we are
dealing with an activity of God which actually has been experienced and which was concretized, as a result of such experience,
in the structure of these psalms . . . a witness to God's activity.[6]

I experience the presence of God, coming powerfully through
the Word, acting on my behalf, not only convincing me that *he*

ANDREW, YOU DIED TOO SOON

can heal me, but I begin to realize that even *now*, God is with me, working, emptying me of sorrow, filling me with his powerful presence, giving new life. *Healing is happening now!* New *trust* comes. I know not how! It is a gift! It is a fresh creation. Out of the ashes of my sorrow God is raising me up. I want to live again. I want to love again. I feel a joy in God's presence as deep as the sorrow. How can I ever thank him enough for this miracle?

> Hope in the Lord!
>> For with the Lord there is steadfast love,
>> and with him is great power to redeem (Ps. 130:7).

> But I trusted in your steadfast love;
>> my heart shall rejoice in your salvation.
> I will sing to the Lord,
>> because he has dealt bountifully with me (Ps. 13:5-6).

God's spirit touched me deeply through these psalms, opening me to pour out deep and honest feelings to God. Such honest praying is the only true prayer, the only way to empty the heaviness of our loss and cast our care upon the Lord. Luther says not to sit and brood, but "lift your eyes . . . take a Psalm . . . and pour out your trouble with tears before God, lamenting and calling upon him. . . . He wills that you should be too weak to bear and overcome such trouble, in order that you may learn to find strength in Him, and that He may be praised through His strength in you. Behold, this is how Christians are made!"[7] The lament psalms opened to me a rich storehouse of God's grace when I was in the depth of sorrow.

Hymns were another treasure. I would sit at the piano, playing and singing, verse after verse, often with tears streaming down my face. And I wondered how authors who lived long ago could have known what I needed in order to pray!

Prayers from our *Lutheran Book of Worship* became another tool for my healing. They are well crafted, giving me words to pray, drawing me to the steadfast love of God.

Thank you, God, for prompting women and men to write—women and men who become your tools for healing me, now when I have no words of my own to pray.

82

Notes

1. Daniel J. Simundson, *Where Is God in My Suffering?* (Minneapolis: Augsburg, 1983), 26–28.

2. Claus Westermann, *The Psalms: Structure, Content, and Message,* trans. Ralph D. Gehrke (Minneapolis: Augsburg, 1980), 29–45.

3. Simundson, *Where Is God?* 27.

4. Simundson, *Where Is God?* 28–29.

5. Westermann, *Psalms,* 40.

6. Westermann, *Psalms,* 58–59.

7. Martin Luther, *Day by Day* (Philadelphia: Fortress Press, 1982), 204.

27.
Home for Easter

Holy Week. We were now five months into our long journey. It was Maundy Thursday. We had eaten and hurried off to church for the service of Holy Communion. It was a wonderful worship.

When the communion service began, ushers moved to the front of the sanctuary. One by one, pews emptied as people stood in the aisle and moved slowly toward the altar.

And there they were, Andrew's friends, home from college. They were standing with their parents, and then kneeling to receive communion together. Herb and I looked at each other. Andrew should be here, too! We felt so cheated. We wanted him. We missed him. All we could do was weep. And the only words we spoke on the way home through our tears were "home for Easter."

28.
At His Grave

We need to go to his grave. Often at first we found flowers, and footprints in the snow. We wondered who had come and what feelings this grave had absorbed.

One beautiful spring Sunday we drove to the cemetery. We sat by Andrew's grave, basking in the warm sun. It was graduation day at Gustavus Adolphus College. Across the open fields we could hear the graduates being called up to receive their diplomas. One by one, their names were spoken. We listened, knowing that Andrew's name would never be one of them.

A large granite stone bears our name. *Chilstrom.* Tall pine trees stand guard around it. Every autumn they give their gift—a luxuriant scattering of pine cones on Andrew's grave.

We, too, will rest there one day. Only God knows when. It is cleansing to go there; heart searching. Because we cannot know if our time on earth will be long or short, there comes new urgency to live life to the fullest when we're there in the presence of that stone and in that quiet place with God. It is a place to pray that God will wash away all sham and deceit, that God will lead us powerfully to do his will. For each day is a gift. We're more aware now of the preciousness of every day. "Life is short and we have not much time for gladdening the hearts of those who travel the way with us. Oh, be swift to love! Make haste to be kind" (Henri-Frederic Amiel, 1821–81).

I had a speaking engagement on September 6. To get there I needed to drive through St. Peter. It was exactly one year after the day we took Andrew to college in the van, loaded up with all of his things. I was reliving that day. As I drove by his dorm, I wished that I could run up and find him there! Instead, I went to his grave. Watering it with my tears, I talked to God. And as I sat pondering, this poem came, and back in the car, I put my words to the page.

Eternity We Share

Andrew, he laughed and loved and felt our feelings.
He hugged and played and needed us.
He reached out to more and more of life
    and now seemingly so far removed.
Can we live without his wit, his smile, his fun, his presence?
If he could enter our grieving now, what would he say?
    "You have life.
    You have things you know you must do.
      Grieve, but go on!
    You have loved me until you have become a part of me;
      That part I take with me to God.
I have loved you until I have become a part of you;
    That is my gift to you for always.
I am alive in you.
You are alive with me in God."
    Eternity we share!

I had gathered up some pine cones, and my hands were sticky. I knew it was time to go, but I was drawn back again and again. I knelt down and, using my fingernail, scratched words in the warm moist earth. *Miss you, Love Mom.*

That night, as I stood at the podium to speak, I still had earth under my nail. I savored it. And the sticky pine cones.

29.
Places of Memory

C ertain places hold memories. Going there brings back the memories and the feelings associated with them. Because of the difficult feelings of grief, we may be tempted to avoid places that we know will trigger these emotions.

Perhaps we need to delay the mourning those places trigger, at least for a time. But ultimately, we will need to go there in order to get on with our grief work. In order to function in certain situations early in the grief process, sometimes we must put our emotions on the back burner. Tough it out. Refuse to feel our feelings. But later, we must examine our emotions up front so that we can get at them to uncap the sorrow and let it flow openly. After a time, we need to lean into the pain.

For us, our lakeside cabin was one of those places of memory. Andrew's presence was everywhere. Water skis. His fishing rod. Games. The screen that he'd broken smashing a mosquito. On a sunny day, I could almost see him standing out in the bay fishing for bass. The cabin has been for us a place of special family times. I dreaded going there even as I longed to go and feel Andrew's presence.

The corner near the high school where I dropped him off on my way to work was another place of memory. Sometimes I felt like stopping there again. One time I actually did. I imagined him getting out of the car, then looking back at me and saying, "Thanks, Mom, I love you."

The bus station where I saw him off for weekends with his friends in St. Peter was another place. Waiting together for Tom or Mark to step off the 5:30 bus. His room. The grave. The place where he died.

Sometimes I felt good going to those places because of sweet memories. Knowing it would hurt. Knowing it would trigger tears. Such encounters with precious places of memory empty the sorrow again and provide a fresh start. And each return moves me a little further along in the journey of grief. Going to those places has been hard, but healing.

30.
I Don't Buy
Pears Anymore

I never imagined how hard it would be to go to the grocery store. Buying food became one of the hardest things I did each week. I never realized what love and care for each member of the family I gave in choosing food.

Usually, when I returned with the groceries, and the garage door went up, Andrew would pop out of the house to help with the bags. He'd perch himself on the kitchen counter while I unloaded the food. He'd be delighted and sit chatting with me while I put everything away.

Pears were Andrew's favorite food. Even when they weren't in season, I'd buy a couple just for him. He loved them. Even now, pushing the cart down the aisle, I stop by the pears, tears rolling down my face. I wanted to buy some. But for what?

One day when I came to the checkout counter, the cashier who had been serving me for years remarked, "You're so slim! Don't you eat?" My slacks had become very loose during the last three months. Grief had left only a little room for food. I had lost twenty pounds. How should I answer?

"My son died in November," I said. "Grief has made my appetite small."

"I'm so sorry," she replied. During those early months it was difficult to be in department stores where I'd shopped with Andrew. Memories of shopping trips overwhelmed me as I wandered down the aisles. I'd stop at the tables of shirts and sweaters, especially if they were in the warm earth tones Andrew had loved. I would pick out a sweater, fingering it, wanting to buy it, tears falling down my face. Then I'd go on, feeling all alone in the store and in the world. Grief is so lonely.

Shopping at Christmastime, with holiday music in the background, still gives me an empty feeling. I am overwhelmed with memories of that first Christmas without Andrew. Rushes of the grief of those first heavy weeks come again and again.

And in the fall, when mothers are scurrying with children to buy school supplies, I am filled with happy memories that also make me feel sad. If I could forget Andrew, I wouldn't need to continue feeling such grief. But I don't ever want to forget him. I am learning to mingle sorrow with joy.

31.
Seeing Someone Who Looks Like Him

Parents who have lost a child tell stories of seeing someone who looks like that child. It's a very emotional experience. Hard to explain. We're not sure what's happening. We stare and don't want to stop. One mother said, "It seems if we look harder, it will be him!"

One Sunday I was the guest preacher and had just begun the sermon. Midsentence, I noticed a young man in the congregation, to the right, halfway back. About eighteen, he sat beside what looked to me like his parents. He looked like Andrew!

My impulse was to stop and stare. Check him out. Of course, I knew with my head that it couldn't be Andrew. But a strange thing happens to a grieving heart, longing for the one who is lost. Your heart, even years later, can't totally believe it. So you continue to search.

I needed to concentrate solely on my preaching and instructed my eyes to avoid even looking in that direction. But later in the service, the young man and his parents came to the altar for communion. I was very conscious of their presence. After serving them communion, I took a few steps back, paused at the corner of the altar rail, turned and looked full face at the young man. His presence felt powerfully like Andrew's. For a moment I just stood there, eyes glued to him. Then I moved on.

The service ended. I drove home alone. My heart emptied. Tears flowed. Andrew, I miss you so deeply!

Sometime later Herb and I were in Riga, Latvia, on a trip for the church. We had been at a dinner arranged for us by our

Latvian hosts. Before parting, we stood conversing in the hotel lobby. My eyes were drawn to four young people in the balcony. One of them looked like Andrew.

I stepped behind the glass of the foyer for an open view to make sure and to satisfy my longing heart. He was broad-shouldered, good-humored, moving among his friends with assurance. My heart was filled with such painful longing. I stared and hoped he didn't notice. No, it wasn't Andrew. But his presence felt like Andrew's.

Then one morning in Minneapolis, I walked into a hotel lobby on business. As I made inquiries of an employee, my eyes were fixed on the design in his tie. Suddenly he interrupted me. "Aren't you Mrs. Chilstrom?"

I looked up. "Mike!" It had been four years since I'd seen him. One of Andrew's best friends. Mike, the friend who'd come for Andrew's football jersey. Mike, who, together with friends, had placed it in his casket at the visitation.

How he had changed! Handsome and twenty-four years old. No longer a teenager, he was a man. A very handsome young man. What Andrew should have been!

He referred me to someone who could help me and said, "I'll be on break in fifteen minutes. I'll wait for you by the front door."

Only part of my mind was on business. And, once it was transacted, I went to the door. There was Mike. Away from his workplace, he created a memorable moment for us. We needed time together, time to catch up with each other's lives.

Later, when I said good-bye and turned toward my car, Mike opened his arms and gathered me into an enormous hug. It felt so good. It felt like an Andrew hug. There in the parking lot, I stood savoring his embrace. He needed to hug me. But I knew also that he'd done it for Andrew.

32.
Letters

Our public life has impacted our grief journey, bringing frequent letters from others in grief, especially bereaved parents. They write to us telling their story, seeking someone to understand and bring comfort. I have welcomed these letters and always send a careful and prayerful reply.

One woman related the tragic story of her son who took his life. Two issues especially troubled her: fear that he might be condemned forever, and her sense that life can never be good again. She apologized for opening old wounds, but begged that I reply. "You know how a mother suffers," she wrote, "and only a mother who has lost a child can understand another mother."

Out of my own grief journey, I replied:

Dear Helen,

I received your June 29th letter. I'm glad you felt free to write to me. Yes, it does open old wounds to read your letter, and yet, I must say the wound stays there, covered by a scar. I will carry it always. No doubt you will too.

The reason I say that I'm glad you wrote is because it's helped you express sad feelings and focus your issues. Also, I want to tell you that I'm happy for the opportunity to share comfort with you that I've been given by many.

I'm so sorry for you in the loss of your dear son. Next week will mark one year and five months since you lost him. Those must have been very hard months for you. How well I know.

You have fears. Fears about whether you will or will not see your son again. Suicide is certainly wrong. And we wonder, Is there forgiveness? Is there any sin too great for God to forgive? If there's forgiveness for anything, it is also for the wrong of suicide, I believe.

My comfort is in God's Covenant, which He made with our Andrew in his baptism, in the Name of the Father, and of the Son, and of the Holy Spirit. "Child of God, you have been sealed by the Holy Spirit and marked with the cross of Christ forever" (*LBW*, 124).

Your son must have had a very hard struggle with depression. Our son did too. Andrew was adopted as an infant and in his teenage years he felt jammed up against a brick wall, confused over who he was. He loved us, his adopted family, very much. But there was a birth mother out there somewhere and he grieved that separation. He needed to meet her in order to know who he was. We were anxious to help him do that. But he was also very much afraid to look for her. He did share his turmoil with us, but we will never know how desperate he must have finally felt, in order to go down that lonely road and take his life. So sad!

Helen, God has promised, "I will never leave you nor forsake you." That promise is for you and for me. That promise also was for your son and mine. I believe God was with them in their dying and brought them safely to be with him forever. I pray that God's Holy Spirit will help you claim it for you and for him every day.

I have come to love Rev. 7:9-17. I've memorized it. I say it in the middle of the night or when I'm driving my car or doing my work. I picture Andrew there.

> . . . I looked, and there was a great multitude that no one could count, from every nation, from all tribes and peoples and languages, standing before the throne and before the Lamb, robed in white, with palm branches in their hands. They cried out in a loud voice, saying, "Salvation belongs to our God who is seated on the throne, and to the Lamb!" And all the angels stood around

the throne and around the elders and the four living creatures, and they fell on their faces before the throne and worshiped God, singing, "Amen! Blessing and glory and wisdom and thanksgiving and honor and power and might be to our God forever and ever! Amen."

Then one of the elders addressed me, saying "Who are these, robed in white, and where have they come from?" I said to him, "Sir, you are the one that knows." Then he said to me, "These are they who have come out of the great ordeal; they have washed their robes and made them white in the blood of the Lamb. For this reason they are before the throne of God, and worship him day and night within his temple, and the one who is seated on the throne will shelter them. They will hunger no more, and thirst no more; the sun will not strike them, nor any scorching heat; for the Lamb at the center of the throne will be their shepherd, and he will guide them to springs of the water of life, and God will wipe away every tear from their eyes."

You wrote, "Life is just not the same anymore." At the death of our sons, we both were like plants cut off at the roots! Just as you, I felt I couldn't live anymore. I felt part of me died, too. But what I have experienced is that I need to go to the cross of Jesus many times a day. More than ever, *I know now why Jesus died for us!* When I feel overwhelmed, I pour out my feelings and pray, "Jesus, will you take the sorrow I feel. I just can't bear it!" Or I pray, "Will you take the fear, it's weighing me down." Or I ask, "Will you take the helplessness I feel, it's crushing me." Or the anger. Or the confusion. Helen, Jesus, "the man of sorrows and acquainted with grief," invites us to cast our cares upon him for we have the promise, "He cares for you." Every time I ask him to take my burden, *I am set free. It's a resurrection.* I pray that it will be also for you.

I remember when I finally began to feel the surge of life return and that I really did want to live. It was like a new creation. A miracle. A gift from God. And then gradually comes fresh courage and an urgency to serve others with this *new gift of life.* For "Those who bear the mark of pain are never really free; they owe a debt to the ones who still suffer" (Anonymous).

You aren't alone. God is with you, loving you as he loved your dear son. He will guide you to the springs of new life now and in heaven forever.

Your friend, Corinne Chilstrom

33.
And How Many Children Do You Have?

I n the early days after Andrew's death, I dreaded having a stranger ask, How many children do you have? I didn't want to say that my son had died. But in telling of my other children, I didn't want to leave Andrew out, either. Because gradually, my feeling of total loss was being replaced with the sense of having him a secure part of me.

One day I was invited to dinner in the home of parents who'd lost an adult daughter. Arriving with me was our guest preacher who didn't know the family well. One of his first questions was, And how many children do you have?

The dreaded question! How would our hostess respond?

I felt sorry that she would need to answer this hard question. Pausing for a moment, she seemed to gather courage. In a strong voice, she enumerated their four living children. And then, confidently, she added, "And then *we have Marion* who died three years ago."

Her wise words etched their way through my confusion. This was my answer. My heart quietly began to recite the fitting response, now my own. "And *we have Andrew* who died."

Andrew *was* a gift. But he is not all lost. He *is* a gift. Present tense. *We have Andrew.* We will always have him. He is a part of the hosts of heaven and he is a part of us.

Unless you have lost a loved one in death, this may be difficult to understand. Robert Cantor said the work of heavy mourning is complete when the lost one "no longer appears as an absence in a barren world but has come to reside securely within one's heart. . . . [There's an] inner presence of the loved one—no longer an idealized hero . . . but a presence with human dimensions. Lost irreversibly in objective time, the person is present in inner time without the pain and bitterness of death. And once the loved one has been accepted in this way, he or she can never again be forcefully removed."[1]

Dr. Alvin Rogness understood it well when he composed these lines after the death of his son:

> He sleeps in a little windswept graveyard
>   on the prairies of South Dakota,
> next to his grandfather and grandmother.

> But he lives on in the fabric of the many
>   lives he cherished, and, I believe, ennobled.

> And with something more that a wistful
>   longing, I believe that he lives
>   and works in another of the far-flung
>   empires over which the Creator rules.

> It is in the dimension of that empire
>   that grief comes tremulously to rest.

Note

1. Robert Chemin Cantor, *And a Time to Live* (New York: Harper & Row, 1978), 66–67.

34.
How Long Does One Grieve?

Nobody understands me at school!"
Julie had been Andrew's high school girlfriend, and lived near us. She stopped in after school one day just to talk. It was two weeks after the funeral, and her friends couldn't understand why she was so depressed. They thought she should be over it by now.

"I knew you'd understand," Julie told me. I did, and invited her to come often. That was the beginning of many after-school visits.

A revealing street survey asked, How long does mourning last after a major loss? The average answer was two to three weeks. If that is the general perception, no wonder we are misunderstood when we grieve! People want us to get back to normal quickly. They expect it. And when we don't, they think something is really wrong with us.

Several hundred widows in London were interviewed, and out of this came a book, *Bereavement*, which has become a classic study about the grief process.[1] I have drawn from this work and others to develop what I see as four distinct stages of grief, but in viewing these, we must sound a word of caution. For each grief is unique. No one should be forced into a grief pattern. We each need our own time and rhythm to grieve well.

The first stage is called *beginning of mourning* and lasts two to three weeks. This period is often marked by emotional outbursts, crying, or laughing. At times the griever may be in shock, feeling

99

emotionally and physically numb. Long muscles tighten and become tense and painful. With grief-induced tightening of muscles, a chemical builds up, which in and of itself causes depression. Exercising releases this chemical. Calisthenics, jogging, swimming, biking are all excellent, but even walking helps.

In order to recognize the reality of the loss, grievers need to tell their story of loss again and again. Listeners are important. Although this stage usually lasts only two to three weeks, it continues to manifest itself on significant days—date of death, birthday, holidays—when the griever relives the initial loss experience.

Searching-Yearning is the second stage, lasting from two weeks to four months. This period is characterized by obsession for the lost one, an almost constant pining and yearning. This obsession may cause insomnia, for by night and by day the griever is searching for the one who has been lost. At night the searching happens in dreams. During the day, grievers frequently describe seeing him in his chair, hearing the key in the door, hearing the garage door go up at 5 P.M., or feeling her beside me. Most grievers who have these experiences will admit they sometimes feel crazy, and say, "There must be something wrong with me."

Reorientation—separating the real from the unreal—is the task that must be accomplished during this difficult stage. Healing comes through supportive and understanding people who listen without judging, who accept the feeling of one who grieves.

Noncompliance is the third stage, beginning around four months. The length of this stage varies greatly. One feels emotionally and physically disorganized and depressed. This shutdown stage, however, is life-saving. For if we continued to grieve at the emotional pitch of the first two stages, the body would be consumed. Depression slows down the racing physiological processes so that bodily organs aren't damaged. If we have not grieved well by expressing feelings before this time, we may find ourselves in serious trouble. Because of an inability to be open to the suggestion of others at this stage, we may turn down invitations to be with friends. That's why it is important for friends to be assertive, drawing the griever back into the mainstream of life.

Well-meaning folks often say, "Call me if I can be of help." But during this stage, the griever may not be able to do so. Grievers need friends to nudge them into action and help them express their needs.

It's hard to be with people when you feel depressed. The pastor I had worked with invited me to lunch during this stage of my grief. When the day came, I felt so depressed that I called and canceled. Wisely, he suspected I didn't want my depression to show. So he responded, "I'm coming over to pick you up." It was important to push me and help me talk. It was just the medicine I needed that day.

The fourth stage, or *watershed*, comes for most adult mourners somewhere between eighteen and twenty-four months. At last the griever realizes there has been a change. A sense of release. A renewal of energy. Renewed ability to make sound decisions. The return of stable eating and sleeping patterns. Once again the griever feels healthy, with a zest for life. One might say that this grief has been resolved.

Except perhaps for those who've lost a child. "Nothing can be harder," I've heard parents say again and again. "When it's your child, your grief never goes away."

When I lost my mother, to whom I was very close, I wept often during the first weeks, but seldom after six months and never after a year. Nothing compares to losing a child. After eight years I continue to grieve. I need to cry my heart out from time to time. And if I don't, grief builds up and becomes destructive.

Note

1. Colin M. Parkes, *Bereavement* (New York: International Universities Press, 1972). The following discussion of the four stages of grief are drawn from pp. 29 ff.

35.
Bottled-Up Grief

I t was December, three years after Andrew had died. We'd moved to a different home, a different city. Periodically, I went out to look for a Christmas tree, but always came home without one.

One evening we were together in the den. Herb said, "Are you angry with me?"

"No," I replied. "Why do you ask?"

"Oh, I don't know. You're just answering me so sharply."

I felt sorry. I didn't understand myself and didn't like what I was doing. But I couldn't seem to stop. It went on for some days until, again, Herb asked me, "Have I done something to hurt you? Do you feel angry?"

By this time the buildup was enormous. There was no use denying it. I burst into tears. And then it all came pouring out. Anger first. But when that layer got spent, the next was sadness. Another Christmas without Andrew. I missed him so!

The first Christmas without him was so painful. He'd been dead for six weeks. Chris and Mary trimmed the tree. Christmas Eve came. The festive table was set, the meal prepared. We sat in the family room waiting. Someone was missing, and it seemed that he should be coming. We all sat motionless. At last we said it. We wanted Andrew. We wept together and helped each other say what needed to be expressed, loving each other as we did so. And finally, we gathered around our Christmas table with his empty chair.

Gradually we learned to make new rituals for Christmas and other holidays. Decorating the archway instead of having a Christmas tree. Baking differently. Cooking differently.

But most of all, we were brutally honest about our feelings. Anger. Sadness. Helplessness. Confusion. Jealousy. Own up to them. Express them. Help each other.

If we bottle up strong feelings and don't get them out, they will certainly come out somehow—perhaps in unexpected ways that will hurt someone badly. I'm sorry, Herb. Even after our promise to be open and honest with each other about our feelings. It's so subtle. I've needed you to be patient and also understanding enough to help press out my painful feelings. Thanks. I have learned anew that it is a responsibility of the griever to be honest with grief feelings. Bottled-up grief is very destructive.

36.
Grief and Illness

The heightened emotions of grieving create enormous stress on the body. Surveys have shown that grievers have a high incidence of visits to physicians and of hospitalizations. For grievers there is a 200 percent above-average new diagnosis of myocardial infarction, a 300 percent above-average incidence of bowel cancer, and a high incidence of death. Why?

It's fascinating to look at the relationship of stress to pathology. We find an identifiable chain reaction from the immediate stressor to the breakdown of the body.[1]

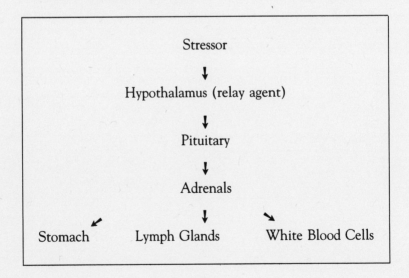

In this case, grief is the stressor. In the center of the brain, the hypothalamus works like a relay agent, sending messages to the endocrine system: "All hands on deck. There's an enemy out there. Stop your routine work and fight the enemy."

Adrenalin goes on emergency status. Blood pressure elevates. The heart pumps more rapidly. Acid secretions overwork in the stomach. Lymph glands cease fighting infection. White blood cell production decreases. All of this affects the ability of the body's immune system to fight infection. The normal defense system is down.

So we see the destructive effects of grief on the body. While grieving, we are physically vulnerable, especially in the case of severe grief over a long period of time. Grievers need relief from the harsh stress of grief, and others can help.

Note

1. This drawing is from Hans Selye, *The Stress of Life* (New York: McGraw Hill, 1976), 99–101.

37.
Fear of
Another Tragedy

Always a confident person, I generally expected good things to happen. When our children learned to drive, for example, I assumed that they would do well. But it was different now! Whenever one of my children went out the door, I felt myself grasping their arm in fear. I couldn't possibly bear another tragedy!

Herb has always been thoughtful about sharing his schedule with me, careful to let me know when he would not be home for dinner. But one evening he was a half hour late. He hadn't called. An hour went by. I felt panic and began calling his staff people. No one answered anywhere. Then I wondered, Was there a staff meeting? I called his secretary and, sure enough, there was. When Herb came home he felt terrible. He thought he'd told me. Neither of us functioned very well during those early weeks of grieving.

Someone told us in a condolence card, "You will dream." We did. Volumes of vivid dreams. So many dreams that I went searching for help in understanding how to interpret them. Several books were helpful. I learned to keep a dream journal, listing the symbols and the feelings. And I learned how to listen to the meaning of my dreams.[1] Later I read Morton Kelsey's *God, Dreams, and Revelation*. That drew it all together, grounding the work in our Christian tradition.

A dream is like having a picture taken of our innermost thoughts and emotions when our guard is down. Journaling the dream is like developing the negative. God does speak to us in our dreams.

I begin journaling a dream by writing the brief drama and then list each symbol and the feelings associated with that symbol. In this process, deep feelings emerge, which relate directly to my life. Aware of these feelings, one can deal with them. Owning feelings is the first step toward healing, for owning them shifts control. I am now in control of my feelings, so they no longer control me. My pattern, at this point in the process, is that journaling becomes a conversation with God, at the cross of Jesus, needing and asking for help. Dreams have been an important part of my healing.

A watershed series of dreams came to me in my third month of grief, while I was still experiencing panic that something might happen to another person in our family.

One such dream had three parts. In the first, I was walking down a hospital corridor with two close friends. Someone had just died, and I felt terribly sad. But my friends seemed unaware that anything had happened.

The second part took place in Old Cairo. We had just returned from there, after leading a retreat for missionaries. The whole city block was desolate, a wasteland of debris. People were sorting through the ruins. I, too, began to look, but nothing was salvageable.

The third part of the dream took me to the corner of a desolate city block. And there to my surprise were four open trunks. Made of wood and newly painted, they were dark green on the outside and pure white inside. The trunks contained pieces of sterling silver—large spoons and pitchers. How valuable, I thought. Someone is sure to steal these. I shut the lids and searched frantically for someone to protect them. Suddenly a slight Mediterranean man stood by my shoulder. His presence calmed me, for I could feel that he cared about that which was valuable in the trunks even more than I did. He moved to the trunks and sat on them. *I knew they were safe.* I knew absolutely, without doubt. When the dream ended, I felt a deep peace.

Until this dream, I didn't know how lonely I had been with my loss, nor how devastated. As if adjusting the lens of a camera, I now had the interior scene of my feelings and emotions in clear focus. Before this dream, I didn't realize what a strange hold the feeling of panic had over me—the fear that someone else in my family would die. The four trunks symbolized the four of us—wide open and vulnerable. Bright green like new growth on tall pine trees stretching confidently toward the heavens. Painted pure white inside—"Though your sins are like scarlet, they shall be like snow" (Isa. 1:18).

Journaling this dream turned into a conversation with God. *Imaging* God beside me, I told him my fears and listened to his response. "For it was you who formed my inward parts; you knit me together in my mother's womb. . . . Your eyes beheld my unformed substance. In your book were written all the days that were formed for me, when none of them as yet existed" (Ps. 139:13, 16). And I heard God valuing the four of us whom he had made, saying, "I want to cleanse you, cluttered with bondage to despair, so that you will be refreshed and revitalized, ready for my use. Valuable and precious. Give me your anxiety. Let me protect the four of you."

The image of the risen Christ was so real I didn't need to search for him. He was already beside me doing his work, loving and protecting us. I was sure. Absolutely sure. And I had peace. It was truly a watershed dream. And a healing.

Note

1. Morton Kelsey's book *God, Dreams, and Revelation* (Minneapolis: Augsburg, 1991) was particularly helpful.

38.
Blaming the Family

Several months after Andrew's death, I was invited to speak at our church's youth convention. Suicide was my topic, and my audience would be six thousand young people. I was torn. How could I bare my deep anguish, experiencing it all over again in such a public forum? But then I asked myself, What if telling my story can save even one of them? And what if I can save some parents a lifetime of unimaginable grieving?

The band on stage was loud, leading the audience in spirited singing as my host led me through the darkened hall. In ten minutes I'd be on. I took my seat in the front row, trembling and praying for courage. The music stopped. An introduction. I took my place in the spotlight. Took a moment to compose myself. Then I told them about suicide—our tragic story. Pleaded with those who felt despair to find a way to live. Told them of the *power in the cross of our risen Lord Jesus.*

That night I hugged scores of kids and heard many secrets. Thoughts of suicide. I was deeply rewarded that night and since, each time young people have come to me or written to me, saying, "Because of your story, I've decided I will never do that!"

Afterward, a young social worker thanked me for my words. He specialized in suicide prevention and was there to lead workshops in his field. I asked him about his work. He said, "Well, the first thing I would say is that kids who think about suicide usually come from troubled families." Indeed, dysfunction in a family system can have serious consequences. But suicide is often much more complex. I felt I had to challenge his simplistic conclusion. "Don't say that to me!" I blurted out.

"Well," he protested, "I don't mean your family."

"Then," I replied, "I will speak for every family you're blaming who carries not only the incredible sorrow of losing a child, but also the terrible burden of blame you place upon us!"

That ended our conversation, and the young man seemed to disappear in the crowd.

Our society has created a stigma against families of those who die by suicide. It is difficult to bear, and I had to know the source. So I studied until I found the answer—right in the history of the Christian church!

During persecutions of the early church, there were many deaths by suicide to escape impending torture. I found death wishes even in the writings of revered church fathers such as Ignatius, who lived in the second century. To stem this tide, Augustine, bishop in North Africa during the fourth century, made a strong declaration against the practice of suicide.

In the Middle Ages, there was another important development. Thomas Aquinas, a leading theologian of the times, declared suicide a mortal sin. This act had a ripple effect upon civil law, causing various punishments for those who died by suicide. Burial in church cemeteries was banned, bodies were dismembered, hearts were cut out, corpses were carried naked through the streets. Even the families of suicides were punished. Their property had to be forfeited to the state. They were left bereaved, isolated, and destitute.

The job of coroner was introduced during the eleventh century in England for the express purpose of finding those deaths that were by suicide, so that the crown could possess the property of the family. *Coroner* means "crown's plea." In all of these ways, for hundreds of years, families of individuals who died by suicide were devastated.

Finally, during the 1930s, Barth, Tillich, Bonhoeffer, and other German theologians began to concern themselves with this societal tragedy. With a single voice they said that while suicide was certainly wrong, if there were forgiveness for anything at all, it surely included suicide, and they declared, "We must begin to care for the survivors."

Society's impulse to blame the family is deeply rooted and has wounded many. I have been wounded and I have met many others similarly hurt. One was a fifty-five-year-old woman who told me her story. When she was in her twenties, she came home from work one day and found her mother hanging dead in their basement. She said that her mother was buried, but she and her father and brother have never, to this day, talked about it.

In the book *Silent Grief*, Christopher Lukas tells his own sad story. Lukas's mother died by suicide when he was six years old. He and his brother were rushed off to relatives. "For ten years the nature of my mother's death was kept a secret from us, though all our relatives and most of their friends knew that she had committed suicide."

The children, of course, attended no funeral or memorial service. Many years later, "at the age of sixteen, my father and I were sitting in a railroad station. . . . I was about to catch the train, and I have always believed my father chose that moment to tell me because he could not bear to hold a prolonged conversation on the subject. 'Why?' I querulously inquired. 'She was sick,' my father replied, making it clear that was all he had to say on the subject. We didn't talk about it again for many years."[1]

After much trauma from unresolved grief, Lukas as an adult went to the literature for help. He found that of some twenty-two hundred works on suicide that have been published since 1965—books, articles, reports in professional journals, theses—only a handful even mention the effects of suicide upon survivors. And he estimated that for every suicide, there are seven to ten close survivors, caught up in this conspiracy of silence, holding in enormous grief.

A "realization, one that was at first puzzling, was how many people, men especially, had not discussed the suicide with family members even years after the event. (In this, as in so many things, I found I was not alone.) By not talking about it, survivors had often not been able to go through some of the normal healing processes. They were 'frozen' in their grief. From my own experiences and from what we have found in our investigations, there seems little doubt that a good deal of the special pain of the survivor/victim is due to this silence, a silence aided and abetted by the reluctance of society to discuss suicide at all."[2]

I was called to a place where there had been several adolescent suicides and asked to speak in a high school auditorium. Part of my presentation focused on my concern over the stigma suffered by surviving families. Lively discussion followed, but the stigma issue never surfaced. I wondered why, because I knew that there were parent survivors in the audience. Afterward, they came to me, quietly and in tears, saying, "What you said is so true. The stigma is terrible. To grieve so deeply and then on top of everything else to feel the blame of your neighbors!"

The bottom line is that all too often society has a simplistic answer for suicide: blame the family. Blaming is more subtle now than in former years, but society still punishes the survivors. For this reason, survivors of suicide continue to tell lies, try to cover the truth, isolate themselves in grief, and remain silent. Some suffer all alone.

Notes

1. Christopher Lukas and Henry M. Seiden, *Silent Grief* (New York: Bantam Books, 1990), pp. 3–4.

2. Lukas and Seiden, *Silent Grief*, 8.

39.
Why Do Suicides Happen?

In addition to the shock and trauma of losing a child to sudden and unexpected death of any sort, parents must deal with particularly heavy issues when the death is by suicide. One wonders. The family wonders. Relatives, friends, neighbors all wonder. Why did this happen? Fear of everlasting condemnation. Vengeance? A dysfunctional family? Mental illness? How could the individual have done it? There's often fear of the place where the suicide occurred. Let's look at these issues.[1]

Families find it extremely difficult when they sense they are being blamed. I have experienced such accusations repeatedly from certain professionals in the social sciences. A young Ph.D. in clinical psychology lectured on the topic of suicide at a training event for pastoral care. Again and again he made the simplistic point that parents are to blame when a child attempts suicide.

Others believe it is always done out of vengeance. A woman sitting in my office at church intended to console me when she said, "Oh, I understand. My son was very rebellious as a teenager, too." I said nothing while she talked on and on. At last I closed the subject. "You don't understand," I said. "It wasn't that way for us."

A friend with five "ideal" children came to comfort me shortly after we had buried Andrew. I was home alone. I welcomed her even as I dreaded the visit. I feared what was about to happen. As we sat over coffee, she began to press me with questions. How did this happen? Why did this happen? Like Job, I felt judged by my friend. It's one thing for the mourner to ask why.

It's quite another thing when someone else asks why. I grew more and more distressed. At last I stood, waited for her to do the same, and walked with her to the door. After she left I exploded with anger. How could she have hurt me so deeply at such a vulnerable time? I needed someone to listen and care, not analyze and judge. I rushed to the phone and called three friends, one after the other, who understood my anger. They listened until my rage subsided.

Like my friend, many people believe there are simple explanations for suicide. One day, for example, Chris came home very angry. He had heard a remark suggesting that Andrew's death by suicide happened because he was mentally ill. "How could they say that about Andrew without even knowing him? I hate having people put Andrew into a category. He was *my brother!*" It hurts deeply when people who don't know you well analyze your family. That's what survivors of suicide are forced to endure.

These experiences sent me on a search. Nothing I had heard about suicide fit Andrew's unique situation. Some of my best help was found in Edwin Shneidman's *Definition of Suicide.*

As a suicidologist, Shneidman has studied hundreds of suicide notes and interviewed those who have attempted suicide unsuccessfully. He now works in the area of suicide prevention. Shneidman categorized these six types of suicide:

1. rational: to escape pain
2. reaction: following loss
3. vengeful: to punish someone
4. manipulative: to thwart someone's plan
5. psychotic: to fulfill a delusion
6. accidental: reconsidered too late[2]

Each person who takes his or her life has a very particular kind of pain, I believe. Our son did. For him his adoption was the big issue and we knew it. The closeness he felt for us in no way erased the bonding he felt to his birth mother. At fourteen, Andrew felt it was important to send for and receive new information about her. For she was the link to his belonging in the world, something he searched for and spoke of often, but never found. After his death we found poems about "going to ancestors of other worlds"; about the "warmth of the womb"; of being "cast forth into the cruel light of day." A tap root of pain for him was "falling out of the procession of generations," blocking out his sense of identity.

Shneidman believes that suicide is an extremely complex phenomenon. Quoting the famous suicidologist, Robert Litman, he says, "There is more to the psychodynamics of suicide than hostility . . . (there is also) rage, guilt, anxiety, dependency . . . predisposing conditions . . . feelings of abandonment, and particularly of helplessness and hopelessness."[3]

Every suicide comes about because of unfulfilled needs, according to Shneidman. Every living system has particular needs. When a person discovers a barrier between a need and its fulfillment, that person attempts either to go around the barrier or take it down. If everything fails, that person attempts to escape. Suicide is not a first choice. Only after the least costly options have been used up, such as restlessness and insomnia, does a person resort to the expensive ones, such as violent outbursts and obsessions. Finally, the individual exits, attempting to stop the "unbearable pain, unendurable anguish, or intolerable emotion . . . the complete stopping of one's consciousness of unendurable pain."[4]

Whatever the basic woundings that lie behind a person's ultimate decision to end life, Shneidman sees these common characteristics in suicide:[5]

1. *Unendurable psychological pain.* It builds until at last a person says, "Too far. No farther."

2. *Unmet needs accumulate with growing frustration.* "Every suicide is logical to the one who decides." Faulty logic, to be sure, but it narrows, at last, to the one remaining option.

3. *A solution is sought to stop consciousness.* Getting very upset even over trivia is critical at this point, especially if something lethal is available.

4. *Helplessness and hopelessness.* A person experiences utter loneliness. "There is nothing I can do and no one can help me."

5. *Ambivalence.* One wants escape but wants life as well. That is why one cries for help. Eighty percent of suicide victims communicate their intention.

In Andrew's case it was one disappointing midterm grade and a turbulent relationship. After stating his intention to go home that weekend in order to take his life, he disappeared. Friends searched the campus frantically. When at last they gave up, they found him back in his room, his usual calm and humorous self. So they didn't worry anymore. If they'd only known better! It is not uncommon, we're told, that once the suicide plan has been made, one feels at peace.

Friends keep confidences, and that is good. But when it is about suicide, a confidence must be broken. Encourage the person to reach out for help. Tell someone! A suicide threat must *never* be kept in confidence!

6. *Constriction* is the process whereby options are lost, narrowing into a kind of tunnel-vision that focuses only on the option of suicide. By this time, with the mind so constricted, one's thinking can no longer even include loved ones who nurture. They are not simply disregarded, Shneidman says. "Worse, they are not even within the range of what is in [the] mind."

When I try to imagine Andrew's pain, I feel ill. The child I cradled and fed. The scratched knees, the fevers, the bruises we mended. And then a pain *this deep!* I still want to fix it but I am so helpless. Forever helpless. Constriction answers for me the question, How could he? the question most survivors ask. But it doesn't ease the pain.

7. *Egression* is the point at which one takes leave from the mind that mediates the intolerable pain. Usually the intense death wish is transient. A short while later, this person would be glad that it did not happen.

My reason for discussing Shneidman's analysis at such length is because it has been profoundly helpful to me. It has been helpful because it fits. It has helped me turn away from the accusing fingers, and freed me from guilt. I cannot stop the accusations, but what I know deep in my heart frees me from accepting their blame. Not that I am guileless as a parent—by no means. But I know that I am not responsible for my son's death.

The physical location of a suicide often haunts survivors. Many express real fear of "the place." Seventy percent of suicides occur in familiar surroundings, at home, or at the place of work.

My early response was that I would never dare to be alone in the house again, that I would want to move. Because I didn't know the reason for his action, I feared the place where Andrew took his life. I sensed a threat of demons hovering there.

After a news article was published about our grief experience, we had many telephone calls from across the country. One was from a man whose seventeen-year-old daughter had taken her life in her bedroom seven months before. He described his fear of that place and admitted that he had never entered her room since her death. He asked, "Did you have such fears?"

Both of us did. Unknown to me until later, Herb made peace with that place the day after Andrew died. He did feel fear and the power of evil. So, first thing in the morning, he deliberately went there to stay alone with God, asking him to deliver our home from the power of evil and to release us from fear. He stayed there until Jesus revealed his presence and brought cleansing and peace and freedom.

The following morning it happened for me. Neighbors had brought in so much food. Taking a hot dish down to my basement freezer, I stopped abruptly when I came to that spot. It seemed sacred and I couldn't step on it. I put down the dish and sat on the floor, weeping, rubbing the carpet, calling out his name, thinking many things. About his life. His pain. His spilling blood. His last breath. I longed for him. Such longing! As I sat there and reflected, all fear went away. I felt God's presence filling that place. I felt God connecting me to Andrew on the other side. It was now a good place.

When I told Herb, he said, "Yes, that happened to me yesterday." Fear in that place was resolved for both of us. In early grief, I went there often to pray, and it became for me a place of comfort.

Notes

1. Much of this chapter draws on my earlier article, "Suicide and Pastoral Care," *Journal of Pastoral Care* 43, no. 3 (Fall 1989): 201–4.

2. Edwin Shneidman, *Definition of Suicide* (New York: John Wiley & Sons, 1985), 29.

3. Shneidman, *Definition of Suicide*, 35.

4. Shneidman, *Definition of Suicide*, 129.

5. Discussion is based on Shneidman, *Definition of Suicide*, 124 ff.

40.
Anger

I saw it welling up in Herb. "Andrew, why did you do it?" He felt so angry at Andrew for taking his life—a life so full of promise. Bright mind. Strong body. Many gifts. He could have accomplished anything he might have wanted to. He'd been given many privileges. And a world full of opportunity was waiting for him.

We knew that Andrew had suffered an identity crisis. Needing to know more about his roots, he pecked out his request on the old Underwood while Herb helped him. Andrew asked Lutheran Social Services of New Jersey for more information about his birth parents. When the response came, Andrew opened the letter as though it were sacred and then went silently to his room. He just needed to be alone. At dinner that evening he said nothing about it. Finally, two days later he asked, "Would you two like to know what was in my letter?" A birth mother talented and sensitive, artistic. A college English major. A birth father macho and into body building. These were deep connections. They described Andrew well. Now he needed to search and find these important connections, and we wanted him to. But there was one problem. Adult adoptees like Andrew, in touch with early feelings, never seem able to envision birth parents as being average. Instead, in adoptees' fantasies their birth parents are either perfect, rich, and famous, or worthless and terrible. And always the deep-seated question that will not go away: *Why did she give me up?*

The last time Herb asked what he thought about searching for his birth mother, Andrew exploded with anger. "She's probably a whore!"

"That's not the picture your letter conveyed," Herb answered. "A sensitive, caring person. A good student. Poetic."

His anger already dissipated, Andrew replied tenderly, "You're right, Dad."

At a party shortly before his death, Andrew was depressed. His friend, Don, suggested they go for a ride. Andrew was thinking about his birth mother. He talked about her. Needed to know her. Don asked, "Are you going to look for her?"

"No. I'm afraid of what I might find." He had closed the door that might have opened his life.

And Herb was angry. True, Andrew was struggling with a lost identity. It was a handicap. But many of us have handicaps. And *one can overcome.* We were there for him. There was a way, and we would find it together. You don't just cop out!

Andrew was very close to Herb. They were soul friends, with communication on a level sometimes beyond words. On their hunting and fishing trips they were never at a loss for things to discuss. Father and son. They loved being together. In a writing class a year before his death, Andrew had written this tribute to Herb:

> My favorite kind of heroes are the ones who don't look like heroes at all. You are convinced that they could never do anything brave, and then they turn around and do something dramatically noble. They don't hide shining suits of armor in their bedroom closet, or a superman costume in their dresser drawer. They just come through in a moment of need and lend a helping hand.
>
> The greatest hero I know is a man named Herb. Raised during the depression in a poor family with eight children, his younger brother was born with handicaps. Although Herb suffered and struggled with this, he learned love, compassion, and patience. Today he still exercises these qualities to his brother and everyone else.
>
> Herb is my favorite hero, not because he is famous, but because he has the biggest heart and the fullest understanding of any father I know.

Along with sadness, anger was continually a part of Herb's grieving. He had to empty out the anger, with family or alone with God on frequent long walks.

Herb identified with Chris, who sometimes felt so angry at Andrew for doing such a stupid thing. "Did he ever have any idea what this would be like for me the rest of my life, without my brother?"

And Herb identified with Andrew's friends who were angry, as well, like Don, the last person Andrew had talked with. They had had a long conversation in the middle of the night. Andrew had been depressed and so he had called Don, a good friend and high school classmate. Before hanging up, Don said, "Will I see you at Thanksgiving?"

"Yes."

The next morning Andrew was dead. Don was so angry! "He was a good friend and he never let me down—until now!" Angry!

"Don't you feel angry?" Herb often asked me. Try as I did, as honestly as I could, I found no anger. Where was my anger? I couldn't feel it. For a long time, the feelings of sadness and helplessness were too overwhelming for anything else to break through.

Instead I thought of raising him for eighteen years with so much caring and sometimes lots of worry. Hurrying for help. Immunizations. Stomachaches. Allergies. Chicken pox. Scratched knees. Knee surgery. Dental work. New permanent teeth knocked flat in a backyard tackle. Brain concussion in his first car accident just after getting his driver's license. Knocked unconscious playing football. Blackouts. DWI. I did everything a mother could do, and was filled with gratitude when the mending happened.

And after all of that, to be so helpless! I was overwhelmed by a longing to have him again. To have him knock on our bedroom door as he always did when allowed to stay out longer than we stayed up, and say, "I'm home, Mom." Or, "Can I come in and talk?"

But that was all over now, and there was nothing I could do. The feelings of longing and helplessness were so enormous that if I felt anger, I couldn't get at it. At least not yet.

That came many months later! I was seen as a resource person to help groups wrestle with the topic of suicide. I struggled to learn and prepare myself. It was always difficult. I had learned too much, and knew more than I ever wanted to know about suicide. But I also felt a responsibility to share it with others. And so, when invited, I spoke at youth conventions and often led seminars and workshops for church or community groups.

One morning, getting ready for one of these missions, I was on my exercycle preparing mind and spirit for a difficult task. I read the Bible passage for the day and made it my prayer. I had learned to be honest with God about my feelings and to cry them out in prayer. For the only real prayer is an honest one. And there it was at last. Anger at Andrew, welling up to overflowing. I shouted it out: "Because of your decision to end your life, Andrew, I'm given these terrible tasks to do! Oh God, I feel so angry!"

Anger. You have to get it out. Even at the dead.

41.
Salt in
My Wound

It was eleven months after Andrew's death. The new chapel was to be dedicated at Luther Northwestern Seminary, my alma mater and a place close to our hearts.

Doodles on his school books and curiosity in conversations leaked periodic clues that Andrew had seminary in the back of his mind. Might he have been a student at this seminary one day? we wondered. It was a joy for us as a family to give the new baptismal font in his memory.

It was a beautiful morning for the dedication. Herb had to go early since he was in the procession. I came from work thrilled about this magnificent place of worship and eager to see for the first time the font we'd given.

Walking into the commons, I met a friend whom I knew well but hadn't seen for some time. Together we walked into the sanctuary.

There inside the tall doors stood the font, elegant and welcoming. Gorgeous brown marble holding a wide square laver. To one side the stately baptismal candle on a marble pedestal. Behind it on the bare brick wall, like a backdrop, five long slender banners in red, black, green, blue, and white. The baptismal waters bubbled, inviting all to remember and renew the covenant God made with us in baptism. I stood, spellbound.

Stepping toward the font, I touched the smooth marble. I felt the cool water and put it on my brow, making a cross. Tears welled up. I didn't try to hold them back.

My friend looked at me and frowned, "I hope you don't do *that* every time you come here!"

My good-hearted, generous, and efficient friend. Helpful and kind. Known for keeping a stiff upper lip when feeling pain. My friend cared about Andrew, I knew, and shared my grief. Yet, she was unable to acknowledge her sorrow and couldn't allow me to express mine.

I felt rejected. For many months I protected myself. I knew that I would not allow my friend to hurt me again, pouring salt into my wound.

But there were others. Others who had tasted the bitter cup of suffering and whose tears had made them lovelier. Others refined in the fires of grief, willing to own and feel harsh emotions. It is they who have grown tender and are able to offer patience and understanding as we grieve. They are the ones who offer balm for our wound. It is they to whom we must go.

Protect yourself from those whose spirit says, I won't allow you to grieve.

42.
Helping the Griever

We are a society with "psychic numbing," according to Douglas John Hall.[1] We have learned to turn off our feelings. To repress suffering is both devastating and dangerous, and there are serious consequences: (1) it becomes difficult to accept or express our own feelings of suffering; (2) we are unable to enter suffering with another or allow others to express their feelings; (3) we look for an enemy, and in our anger we project our pain onto another.

When we grieve, we can do things to help ourselves. But we also need others to do certain things for us. I'll make a list:

1. *Get in touch.* Run to the griever. It's urgent in the event of sudden loss. We need someone to help hold our world together until we can realize and make sense out of what has happened. Your presence is important. Not your words. Just being there. Hug us who grieve. Weep with us. Pray with us.

2. *Listen.* Words don't help a griever much. We can't listen well. Advice is mostly harmful. What we really need is that you listen. We need to tell our story over and over. Our story changes, because in good grieving, there is movement. It is a process, a journey.

Frederick Buechner said grief is like having your house burn down.[2] It takes a long time before you know all you've lost. When you help us tell our story again and again, we're able to do our work of grieving. It's in the telling that we gradually realize what we've lost, and healing is happening.

125

3. *Stay in touch.* Continue over the months (and years) to draw out our feelings. Grief is not one big thing; it has many pieces. And every day when you meet us on our grief journey, you'll find us dealing with one more piece. It may be new. It may be old. And there are many feelings that go with those pieces.

Because I've learned this the hard way, I often approach a grieving person by asking, "How are you doing?" or "What's going on with you today?" It's one way to get at the piece and the feelings that go with it. But an even better way of drawing it out, I've learned, is to ask specifically, "What is the heaviest, hardest thing you're dealing with right now?" Grievers know, and they're often quick to respond. We grievers can tell you. And we will, if we believe that you won't judge us and that you really care. You will be a messenger from God for us. If you will listen, you will lighten our burden, relieve our stress. And our health will be better for your ministry to us.

4. *Give practical help.* Early in grief, we need you to tell us when to eat and drink. To bring us food. Do errands. Drive for us. Help us get exercise. Go with us for a walk. We need to loosen tense muscles. And later, help us tell you what we need. Maybe we need help with cleaning the house at a time when we still can't function or write thank-you notes and letters.

5. *Share memories.* We want to talk of our loved one who died. You won't offend us when you mention that person's name. It's so special now after eight years when someone still writes and speaks of Andrew. Sharing memories, telling funny stories, looking at pictures are good ways to work through grief, especially for children. And with the pictures and the memories, feelings begin to surface. It's healing.

6. *Share silence.* When grief is fresh and the mind is confused, it's impossible to listen to lots of words. Grievers have to talk out their feelings and need silence to sort out their thoughts. Silence is necessary to focus and transform thoughts into words. Your silent presence is helpful.

7. *Help us return to our social life and work.* It was two weeks after Andrew's death. Herb wondered how he could begin to

work again. He dreaded facing the public. He had a preaching assignment in a Minneapolis church that he hadn't canceled. He decided he should ease back into work. I went with him. Looking at him up in the chancel, I saw the drawn face of a very sad man. What were his feelings as he faced one of the congregations in his care for the first time after his son had died by suicide? Everyone knew of our tragedy.

He ascended the pulpit. He spoke honest words about our loss and then preached a powerful sermon. At the close of the service, during the recessional, the pastor of the parish beckoned me to join him and Herb so his people could greet us together. They came, not condemning, but with hugs and love, some saying, "I lost a son, too."

At dinner with the pastor and his family, we were given a very special gift. Love and understanding. Our wounds were soothed with healing balm. They will never know how wonderful it was to be in their church and their home that difficult day. They helped us bridge the dreaded chasm between our own grief and going back to work. It was a day of healing.

8. *Bring the griever to worship.* Allowing God to nurture us regularly through word and sacrament fortifies our relationship with God. We experience in the most personal way that the promises of God are true, that our God is one of steadfast love and faithfulness. Hymns and God's promises fill our reservoir in worship, saved up, as it were, for the time of crisis. The continued fellowship of worship encourages us and shores us up for difficult days that are sure to come. But when the time of grief and separation does come, it is often very difficult for us to go to worship, especially alone. It's helpful when someone understands this need and offers to go with the griever to worship.

It is a responsibility to grieve well. The goal of grief is to acknowledge the change that has occurred, to integrate the change, and to begin a new life. My head knew that Andrew had died, but my heart wouldn't believe it. The journey of grief is *helping the heart know what the head knows. You can help.*

ANDREW, YOU DIED TOO SOON

Notes

1. Douglas John Hall, *God and Human Suffering* (Minneapolis: Augsburg, 1986), 42–47.

2. Frederick Buechner, *Sacred Journey* (New York: Harper & Row, 1982), 41.

c

43.
Grieve and
Live Again

The day Andrew died I remember saying, "I can't live without him!" Eighteen years of mothering him seemed totally wasted. I felt it was useless to go on.

"But think of all the happy memories," someone said. "They will outweigh your sense of loss." It made no sense to me then. I wanted Andrew, not just memories.

The only way to avoid grief is not to have loved. To love means to be deeply attached, thus vulnerable and open to great sorrow in loss. It was Colin Parkes who said that grief is the price we pay for love.[1]

In those early weeks of grieving, I tried to get back into the routine of life, but every day seemed like a mountain to conquer. One morning as we dressed, Herb said, "If it could only be a nightmare. I wish I could jump over the next months; this grief feels too heavy day after day." Even though we shared the same grief, it still seemed that we each carried it alone. We never knew how lonely or how heavy grief could be.

One of the letters in the cake pan helped to sustain us. It was from Al and Nora Rogness. We read it often. Day after day in our struggle their words lifted and encouraged us:

Dear Herb and Corinne,

Yesterday we learned of Andrew's death. It is twenty-four years since our Paul was struck down by a truck to die instantly. He would now have been forty-eight. When a son or daughter of our friends dies suddenly, still young, some of the pain of long ago surfaces again. We know the wrenching hurt. It won't go away quickly, never really. Some of life's mirth is gone. . . .

We . . . struggled with guilt. Had we only known that his life would be cut short, what more should we have done for him? This was a dead-end street. Moreover, I rather quickly fell back on the sweeping, overwhelming forgiveness of our Lord. He had forgiven and forgotten any lack in us, or in Paul. The terrain was swept clean, and we could "lay aside every weight" and run the race. It helped me to see Paul in the bleachers among "the cloud of witnesses" cheering me on to drop any guilt, and even grief, to return to the common life with joy and zest.

It was never easy. I had never known such wrenching pain. For weeks, even months, when I wasn't pressed with tasks, Paul would surface. Sometimes it seemed that it was my duty to grieve; if I didn't grieve, had I really loved him? I was not grieving for Paul who now was safe in the hands of his Lord, spared the troubles that a longer life may have given him. Of course, I was saddened to think that he might have been of service to his Lord those added years. But I was grieving for myself, this I realized.

Nothing anyone can say at this moment will remove the deep hurt. God himself will need time to do this for you. Each of you, though grieving together, is driven out upon an island. As George MacDonald said, "even when we weep together, we are two."

Our hearts bleed for you.

It does take time. Working through the grief of losing a child is a long, hard journey. But, wrote parents from North Carolina who had also lost a son by suicide just before his college graduation, "One morning you'll wake up and realize you didn't cry all day yesterday. It takes a very long time. Three months is just the beginning. Do not push yourselves. Do not worry what others think. Try not to punish yourselves."

John C. Raines reminds us that grief is a friend who helps us remember and own the past with its shadows. And having done that, we're able to enter our new future.

Just as grief preserves the meaningfulness of the past, it also opens us—slowly—to a new future. Grief is a midwife; it lets the journey continue. Often after a profound and shattering loss, we think that we will never be able to live again. For awhile we think that life will now be always gray, though we may "go on," the journey of our life is forever diminished. We may think that to want to live again and to know satisfaction again is to abandon the past. Grief slowly gives us permission to say Yes to life, to want life, to think that we deserve life. [2]

This has been my experience—grief is a good friend, preserving past memories so that we are born into a new future. When I felt that I couldn't live again, grief was the friend that slowly gave me permission to say Yes to life, to want to live.

Sadness and self-pity happen to us; sorrow is something "we do" to get our lives moving again. We can choose to stay mired in sadness. Without realizing what we're doing, we can choose not to live again or love again. Because living and loving opens us to the possibility of further loss. Dare we be vulnerable again? It takes courage to grieve well. It takes courage to choose to live again.

The emotions necessary for grieving are painful. But we will find great power in the process. We enter the journey wounded. But the journey of good grieving is movement toward healing and wholeness.

One spring day, expecting guests, I went to Andrew's room to make up his bed. I was seized with the need for him. It was for him I wanted to be preparing this bed. I stopped to grieve. I sat down in the chair crying out to God: "Will you take the sorrow I feel and the helplessness? I cannot bear it! Lord Jesus, let my sorrow die with you at the cross. Take the burden as you have promised and raise me to newness of life."

"Gradually hope comes through," says Granger E. Westberg in *Good Grief.*

We need not be afraid of the real world. We can live in it again. We can even love it again. For a time we thought there was nothing about life we could affirm. Now the dark clouds are beginning to break up and occasionally for brief moments rays of sun come through. And hope, based on faith in a God whom our

131

fathers (and mothers) have found to be dependable, once more becomes a part of our own outlook on life.[3]

Movement from brokenness to wholeness comes through the cross of our risen Lord. We are lifted from death to life. New life. Day after day. Bit by bit. I remember the day when I began to feel the surge of life again. I really *did want to live.* A creation miracle.

We can know happiness again! Raines calls it "seasoned happiness," a "happiness with shadows." And with that new life-surge, one begins to think not only about what has been lost, but increasingly to feel grateful for the gift one has had. I haven't forgotten Andrew. I think of him daily and dream of him often. I have lost his physical presence. But his life continues to be a part of me. I do have him.

Grief is a root experience. We've been cut off at the root, and a new life forms. A very different life, perhaps. We learn gradually to become friends with our *new self,* the wounded self, the scarred self, but a more courageous self. We can learn to love that changed person.

> *Scars*
> There might always be
>   a scar
>   or blemish—
> Reminder of weakness
>   and pain past—
> but healing, time . . .
>   bring us to a point . . .
> We forget it shows. (Julie Beck)

Grieving unlocks strong emotions, releasing anger, self-pity, and other forces that can destroy us and distance us from God and others. Into the wasteland of our loss, into that emptiness comes new life with the gift of compassion. A compassion that senses the sorrow of others and throws them a lifeline. The compassion that has been given to us reaches out through us to others. Grief is good. Grief is a friend. So grieve well.

Out of darkness
  shall come dawn,
Out of winter
  shall come spring,
Out of striving
  shall come peace,
Not by our power,
But by the power
  of God. (Anonymous)

Grieve, and live again!

Notes

1. Colin M. Parkes, *Bereavement* (New York: International Universities Press, 1972), 5.

2. John C. Raines, "The Goodness of Grief," *Christian Century* (October 1986): 886.

3. Raines, "The Goodness of Grief," 886.

4. Granger E. Westberg, *Good Grief* (Philadelphia: Fortress Press, 1971), 64.

5. Raines, "The Goodness of Grief," 887.

Appendix

[This meditation was preached at the funeral for Andrew John Chilstrom on November 14, 1984 by the Rev. Dennis J. Johnson.]

Let not your hearts be troubled; believe in God, believe also in me. In my Father's house are many rooms; if it were not so, would I have told you that I go to prepare a place for you? And when I go and prepare a place for you, I will come again and will take you to myself, that where I am you may be also . . . I will pray the Father and he will give you another Counselor, to be with you forever, even the Spirit of truth . . . I will not leave you desolate; I will come to you (John 14:1-3, 16-18).

Herb and Corinne, we are here today to do for you what you have done so often for so many of us. You have stood with many of us in dark days. You have put your arms around us and shared our hurt and pain. You have spoken words of comfort and hope to us.

Today, we try to do for you, for Mary, and for Chris what you have done for us. We stand with you. We put our arms around you and cry with you. We haltingly try to find the right words.

We, too, ask the question that won't go away, Why?

What would cause a handsome, gifted young man to choose not to live—a young man who had a good relationship with his parents, who had friends and a belief in God? We wonder . . .

What pressures did no one know about? What social influences were present? What ideas came to him? Did he somehow mistake the loneliness that all people feel as something special within him? Did he somehow feel that his weaknesses were not common to all humanity? Did he feel that his problems could not be worked through? Did his anger at the uprootedness represented by adoption overwhelm him? Was it simply his unusual fascination with death and what lay on the other side of life's greatest mystery that made him impatient for an answer? Was it something physical—an altered body chemistry that figured in a depression he could not shake? Did he not know that there was a twenty-year-old, a thirty-year-old, a forty-year-old person within him who deserved a chance to be?

We ask so much and know so little. We search for psychological understanding—and there is little that helps. We search for sociological understanding and take no comfort from our knowledge that suicide is a leading cause of death for this age group, that it is not just an individual problem but societal as well.

There is no place to turn. It scares us. Is there nothing that we can do to prevent this from happening? If our knowledge of psychology cannot prevent it—if good parenting is not a guarantee, if our faith and prayers do not provide protection—then all of the answers to which we look have failed. And the darkness has indeed surrounded us.

Herb, you have never led us down a false path by preaching to us a theology of glory. You have never told us that if we have faith, everything will go right in life. You have preached a theology of the cross. God meets us in this cross. Here God makes himself present, hidden in weakness, vulnerable, suffering, forsaken, dying.

In the abyss of despair, in the deepest darkness, God comes. In the painful reality of our mortality, our ultimate loneliness, our brokenness, God encounters us. By God's Holy Spirit—this Counselor, Comforter—we are enabled to see the cross as God's embrace. God enters our darkness and embraces us with total and unconditional acceptance, identifying completely with the pain and sorrow of our existence. The questions continue, but when the questions are asked at the foot of the cross—when our anger and tears are directed toward this cross—healing begins. Here we are made free—free from guilt of self-accusations, free from fear of the judgments of others, free from the need to seek any other justification for our lives other than His. In the darkness, we see the cross and we feel its naked and raw power. The beginning of hope is to hope only in God. It is not to hope in our righteousness or in our knowledge or in our right solutions to problems, but to hope in God *alone*.

135

Will the hurt ever recede to the point where it will be possible to celebrate Andrew's life—to remember chiefly what was beautiful in him? Can God's hope break through the confusion, the anger, and the hurt? Is it possible that the grief can be healed? (With humans it is impossible, but with God all things are possible.) Jesus has promised, "I will not leave you desolate. The Spirit—the Counselor, the Comforter—will come." The Spirit is working even now—through the Word, through family and friends, through sorrow itself—to heal.

Herb and Corinne, Mary and Chris, we wish we could spare you from blaming yourselves. We hope you will be as compassionate to yourselves as you are to others.

I want to share with you a letter written by a Catholic priest, Father Arnaldo Paugrazzi. His words summarize the thoughts that parents have in the months following such a death. I share them in the hope that these words will be helpful to you, but also that they might serve as words of prevention to others:

My dear child,

As you read this letter, we would like you to know that we miss you and that so much has changed because of you. We always thought this sort of thing happened to other people, not us. Maybe in your heart, you thought you were doing us a favor by taking your own life.

What hurts most is that you never really said good-bye or gave us a chance to say good-bye to you. Our eyes have been filled with tears as we've tried to change what has been, tried to understand your despair, your mystery.

At times, we have been angry with you for what you did to yourself, for what you did to us. At times, we've felt responsible for your death. We've searched for what we did or failed to do—for the clues we missed.

Yet we also know that, no matter what, we couldn't choose for you. We are learning to stop feeling responsible for your death. If we were responsible for you, you'd still be alive!

We all think of you so often, even when it hurts to remember. We are lonely for your presence and whenever we hear your songs, we still cry for you. We feel sad that you're not here to share so many events with us. That's when our mornings have no beginnings and our nights seem long as winter.

Slowly, though, it's getting less hard. We try to remember the good times. Maybe, we are seen smiling a little more. Yes, we are learning to live again, realizing that we cannot die because you chose to die.

We pray that you are at peace. At the end of our days, we look forward to being with you again. Peace.[1]

Healing will come—slowly. The Spirit will be your Counselor. The Spirit will come to you and the Peace of Christ will be yours.

Now, we must commend Andrew to the care of this loving God who suffers with His people. We claim for Andrew the justification that is the free gift to all of God's people—"for there is no condemnation for those who are in Christ Jesus." We commend him to God who washed him in baptism eighteen years ago in New Jersey, when God accepted him without merit— "Andrew, child of God, you have been sealed by the Holy Spirit and marked with the cross of Christ forever." In baptism, God made a covenant of steadfast love, a stubborn love that never quits, that doesn't end, not even in death.

In John's Gospel, Jesus says, "In my Father's house are many mansions, I go to prepare a place for you."

Using this same imagery, perhaps we can say Andrew chose to enter before his place was ready. But our Lord, who numbered the hairs on his head, who bought him with a price, who redeemed him and called him by name, will not turn him away. As a good host faced with an unexpected guest, he hastily makes the preparation with pain in his heart for the manner in which he came and pain for the agony of parents and family, but with an ocean of love for Andrew.

Now we must bury Andrew, but we will not forget that we will bury him in Resurrection Cemetery. Resurrection is our hope. We proclaim that death does not have the final word. Our Lord Jesus Christ is the final word and he says, "Behold, I make all things new!"

ANDREW, YOU DIED TOO SOON

As we look forward to resurrection, our future hope informs the present moment. Because of resurrection and that promise to make all things new, we affirm that this life is filled with possibilities. In spite of all its pain and struggle, life is worth living. We must not lose sight of our conviction that life is a gift, a beautiful gift to be nourished and respected and used for the enhancement of all life. So we will continue to proclaim the gospel, the good news. We will continue to invite young men and women to join us in following the Lord of life: to give our lives in working for a better world; in fighting despair and loneliness; in binding up the wounds of the hurting; in nurturing children and giving them hope; in caring for the disadvantaged; in working for peace, the peace of the whole world; in refusing to accept the nuclear madness and destruction of this planet.

Let us give ourselves to protecting the gift of life, life as God has given it to us. This is to embrace a life worth living. As we do so—as we move through the years that are ahead—we will do so with two essential prayers: the first is the ancient Kyrie of the church, "Lord, have mercy" (for we are all beggars in life and we shall remain so); and the second is: "Thanks be to God who gives us the victory through Jesus Christ, our Lord." Amen.

Note

1. The Rev. Arnaldo Paugrazzi, published in *Context*, (March 1984): 2.

Bibliography

Brodinsky, David M., and Schecter, Marshall D. *The Psychology of Adoption*. New York: Oxford University Press, 1990.

Buechner, Frederick. *Sacred Journey*. New York: Harper & Row, 1982.

Cantor, Robert Chernin. *And a Time to Live*. New York: Harper & Row, 1978.

Davidson, Glen. *Understanding Mourning*. Minneapolis: Augsburg, 1984.

Hall, Douglas John. *God and Human Suffering*. Minneapolis: Augsburg, 1986.

Hewett, John J. *After Suicide*. Wayne Oates, ed. Philadelphia: Westminster Press, 1980.

Hodge, J. R. "They that Mourn," *Journal of Religion and Health* 2 (1972): 229–40.

Kelsey, Morton. *God, Dreams, and Revelation*. Minneapolis: Augsburg, 1991.

Lifton, Betty Jean. *Lost and Found*. New York: Harper & Row, 1988.

Lukas, Christopher, and Seiden, Henry M. *Silent Grief*. New York: Bantam Books, 1990.

Luther, Martin. *Day by Day*. Philadelphia: Fortress Press, 1982.

Luther's Works. Vol. 54, *Table Talk*. Edited by Theodore G. Tappert. Philadelphia: Fortress Press, 1967.

Lutheran Book of Worship. Minneapolis: Augsburg, 1978.

The New Oxford Annotated Bible. New York: Oxford University Press, 1991.

Nouwen, Henri J. M. *Reaching Out*. New York: Doubleday, 1975.

Parkes, Colin M. *Bereavement*. New York: International Universities Press, 1972.

ANDREW, YOU DIED TOO SOON

Raines, John C. "The Goodness of Grief," *Christian Century.* 15
October 1986, 886–87.

Romstad, Paul O. "Funerals," *Lutheran Standard.* March 1986,
p. 16.

Selye, Hans. *The Stress of Life.* New York: McGraw Hill, 1976.

Shneidman, Edwin. *Definition of Suicide.* New York: John Wiley
& Sons, 1985.

Simundson, Daniel J. *Where Is God in My Suffering?* Minneapolis:
Augsburg, 1983.

Sorowsky, Arthur D., Baran, Annette, and Pannor, Rueben. *The
Adoption Triangle.* Garden City, N.Y.: Anchor Press, 1971.

Westberg, Granger E. *Good Grief.* Philadelphia: Fortress Press,
1971.

Westermann, Claus. *The Psalms: Structure, Content, and Message.*
Translated by Ralph D. Gehrke. Minneapolis: Augsburg, 1980.